INNER
TREASURES

INNER
TREASURES

Swami Chidvilasananda

A SIDDHA YOGA PUBLICATION
PUBLISHED BY SYDA FOUNDATION

Every heart blazes with divine light.
Every heart trembles with divine love.
Even if a person is unaware of his own yearning,
every human being is constantly engaged
in the pursuit of lasting happiness,
profound peace, and unconditional love.

SWAMI CHIDVILASANANDA

Published by SYDA Foundation
371 Brickman Rd., South Fallsburg, New York 12779, USA

Acknowledgments
Grateful appreciation goes to Marilyn Goldin for preparing the talks for publication,
to Hemananda for her invaluable editorial assistance, to Diane Fast for copy-editing,
to Eileen Considine, Judith Levi, and Dana Nellen for proofing the text,
to Cheryl Crawford for design, to Stéphane Dehais for typesetting,
to Leesa Stanion for compiling the index, and to Cynthia Kline,
Valerie Sensabaugh, Osnat Shurer, and Sushila Traverse
for overseeing the production of this book.

Swami Kripananda

First published 1995
Printed in the United States of America

Permissions appear on page 83.

Library of Congress Cataloging-in-Publication Data
Chidvilasananda, Gurumayi.
    Inner treasures / Swami Chidvilasananda.
        p.   cm.
    "A Siddha Yoga publication."
    ISBN 0-911307-41-9 (pbk.)
    1. Spiritual life—Hinduism.   I. Title.
BL1237.36.C54   1995
294.5'44—dc20   95-41464
                                                      CIP

CONTENTS

NOTE ON SANSKRIT TERMS

Sanskrit terms and scriptural excerpts quoted in the talks are given in a slightly modified version of the international standard system, to enable the reader to distinguish the pronunciation easily. Thus *ś* is written as *śh*, *ṣ* appears as *ṣh*, *c* is shown as *ch*, and the semi-vowel *ṛ* is written as *ṛi*.

For the convenience of the reader, well-known Sanskrit terms that come within the body of a paragraph appear as regular text. Less familiar terms are in italics with diacritical marks to distinguish the long vowels.

Further information on Sanskrit terms in the text can be found in the Glossary, which also shows the correct pronunciation of each word. A general guide to Sanskrit pronunciation accompanies the Glossary.

INTRODUCTION

Imagine the scene: It is the last week of the year, and the mountain air is clear and very cold. The Christmas retreat at the Siddha Yoga ashram in South Fallsburg, New York, has begun, and the high point of each day's program comes in the evening, when participants gather for a talk given by Shri Swami Chidvilasananda, better known as Gurumayi. Outdoors, I join the group and we move quickly, bracing ourselves against the chill, but once inside the meditation hall, a coziness envelops us. Many hundreds of people fill the huge hall—in former times it was the ballroom of a Catskills hotel—and yet it feels intimate, as if we are in someone's living room, huddled comfortably around a fire. At the same time, it is as though the whole universe were crystalized into that one spot, so expansive and powerfully charged is the atmosphere.

The four talks reprinted in this volume were delivered during the 1994 Christmas retreat, and their titles reflect themes of the season: "The Mirror of God," "The Sadhana of Joy," "The Sadhana of Peace," and "The Sadhana of Love." Here Gurumayi teaches that such lofty goals are indeed within our reach, but that first it is necessary to address certain basic human problems. Some of these problems are indeed so basic that they may not even be recognized as such, for often we assume incorrectly that they are natural ways of being. With beautiful lyricism, she discusses solutions from the highest and subtlest viewpoint. She recites, even sings, verses from scriptures that make us feel expansive, feel that anything is possible, that no problematic situation is too great to overcome, and then—before we can lapse back, shrink back to the ordinary consciousness that calls this too lofty, too idealistic, some pretty advice for a hermit on a mountaintop but not for me—this is when Gurumayi impresses upon us the necessity of practical solutions, practical implementations of exquisite theory. For indeed, effective *sādhana*, or spiritual practice, entails not so much contemplating the goal as implementing and thus experiencing tastes of the goal along the way. Joy and peace and love, Gurumayi emphasizes, already exist within us. As we engage ourselves in the practice of these qualities, we can begin to experience their actual presence, with astounding immediacy.

Gurumayi draws upon the wisdom and advice of ancient sages, of contemporary teachers, of her own spiritual master, Swami Muktananda, and perhaps most potent of all, her own experiences. She has attained the same truth that was known by the sages who articulated it in scripture. When she offers solutions to time-worn problems, it is with the authority of one who knows, who has, in the terminology of Kashmir Shaivism, gone through the process of transformation from limitation to divine, infinitely expanded consciousness.

In order to illustrate the nature of that consciousness and how to experience it, Gurumayi draws upon the words of the scriptures, in keeping with the ancient Sanskritic tradition of transmitting sacred knowledge. The use of scripture for illustration is two-fold: First, the articulation of revelatory experiences recorded by the sages provides an intellectual springboard from which to contemplate supreme truth. Second, Indic religious traditions hold that sacred texts are composed from within a state of divine insight and revelation, and therefore by reading, listening to, or reciting these works, the spiritual aspirant can tap into that divine source and even experience it directly, according to his or her particular level of preparation and awareness.

Gurumayi quotes from the rich tradition of India as well as from the writings of mystics from around the world. In a certain sense, then, she is heir to all great spiritual traditions. But more specifically, she is recognized in the Siddha tradition in India as having arrived at the place, the state where to know God is to embody all divine truth in one's own consciousness. In Kashmir Shaivism, this "place" is called *anupāya*, that is, the place beyond the (spiritual) path: the *sādhaka*, or spiritual aspirant, has reached the end of the road, the summit, the state in which there is no more path to travel. A being with such awareness is said to have attained *svātantrya*, absolute freedom, and thus is free to tread either no path, or any path at all, just for the delightful play (*vilāsa*) of it.

In the tradition of the *siddhas*, the Guru is recognized as the embodiment of the grace of God, and therefore it is the Guru who oversees the *sādhaka's* transformation, infusing it with divine grace. The tradition recognizes that because their source is in transcendent, universal consciousness, the methods and suggestions of the Guru may be difficult to comprehend from an ordinary, limited state of consciousness. Just consider the stories of *avadhūts*, great yogis who have completely transcended ordinary body consciousness, ever established in the universal: they are simultaneously delightful, inspiring, and most perplexing. Encountering the extraordinary behavior of an *avadhūt*, the seeker must leap beyond every conventional mode of interpreting information. The Siddha Gurus, often adopting a much more "normal" appearance, nonetheless offer advice that may be incomprehensible until one contemplates the truth from which it originates. In either case, by taking refuge in a truly realized being, the aspirant receives guidance in how to progress with *sādhana*, as well as the divine grace to support the process.

Gurumayi has been the spiritual master to many thousands of aspirants worldwide for well over a decade. The position of authority in the Siddha Yoga lineage was transmitted to her by her master, the renowned *siddha* Swami Muktananda Paramahamsa (1908-1982). Muktananda, whose extraordinary journey of spiritual awakening covered many years and many miles across the vast land of India, always claimed that he owed the perfection of his *sādhana* to the grace of his spiritual master, the greatly revered *siddha* and indeed *avadhūt* Bhagawan Nityananda. In the same way, Gurumayi speaks constantly of the transformative grace bestowed upon her by her own master.

In the Siddha tradition, Bhagawan Nityananda, Swami Muktananda, and Swami Chidvilasananda are all recognized as embodiments of the same Truth, the same divine consciousness. And yet, each is recognized as exhibiting a unique personality and sensibility in conveying the teachings, in giving *śaktipāt* (the transmission of divine energy), and in nurturing devotees in their quests for perfection. These three Siddha Gurus may be seen as representing an ancient pattern by which earlier lineages have evolved. I am reminded of the great masters of Kashmir Shaivism of over one thousand years ago, when the three magnificent *siddhas* Somananda, Utpaladeva, and Abhinavagupta established and set into motion the Pratyabhijñā School. Each left a distinct imprint, appropriate for the spiritual and intellectual conditions of his time, and according to his individual personality and temperament as a spiritual leader. The three are generally recognized by scholars as the founder, the systematizer, and the expounder of the Pratyabhijñā tradition.[1]

---

[1] These particular labels were first designated by R.K. Kaw in *The Doctrine of Recognition (Pratyabhijñā Philosophy)* (Hoshiarpur, India: Vishveshvaranand Institute, 1967; Vishveshvaranand Indological Series, No. 40), pp. 49-60.

The lineage of *siddhas* stretches back through the ages, but in this century we might say that the "founder" of the present Siddha Yoga lineage was Bhagawan Nityananda (d. 1961), whose immense *śakti* (spiritual power) attracted devotees to make their way through the untamed jungle in order to receive the *darśan* (auspicious glance) of this mysterious *siddha* in a simple ashram on the outskirts of the virtually unknown village of Ganeshpuri. There was no "system" as such, until Nityananda instructed his disciple Muktananda that the time was approaching when many thousands of seekers, far beyond even the shores of India, would be given the previously all-but-impossible opportunity to receive the *śaktipāt* initiation, and that Muktananda should provide a system for this to happen. What followed was the establishment of many ashrams and meditation centers, the institution of the "Intensive" (a formalized setting in which the transmission of spiritual energy could take place), and dozens of books of poetry, philosophy, scriptural exegesis, and a spiritual autobiography—a sharp contrast to the laconic style of Nityananda!

The *siddha* known as the "expounder" of the Pratyabhijñā School was Abhinavagupta, for it was he who inherited the potent nugget of truth that had been systematized in such a way as to provide a matrix of teachings with which the seeker could advance and understand the philosophical foundation of his *sādhana*. Given this, Abhinavagupta launched into unearthing the most sublime variegations of this knowledge; he embellished it, he penetrated the very finest points of how supreme consciousness becomes manifest in the world. This led to an extremely subtle investigation into the fine arts—according to Abhinavagupta, artistic expression is a natural link to divine knowledge—and his work became the cornerstone of Indian aesthetic theory. The mysterious process of creativity is evident here, in the progressive revelation of a sacred truth through the elegant unfolding of a spiritual tradition. Other creative endeavors follow a similar pattern. With dance, for example, the performer must first receive the inspiration for movement; next follows the meticulous mastery of the steps; and finally, having become one with the initial energy as well as with the particulars of its formed expression, the dancer is free to delve into the intricacies of the performance with creative embellishment, fine-tuning and ornamenting, experimenting, and joyfully soaring in the pure creative atmosphere of exquisite, divine play. Is it any wonder that Muktananda bestowed upon his future successor the spiritual name of Chidvilasananda, "the bliss of the play of consciousness"?

Firmly established in that supreme state of divine awareness, Gurumayi reaches out in endless ways to assist seekers in attaining that perfection. Throughout her talks, she returns to the message to look within, where perfection lies, for then we will not be cast about by external conditions: "Only perfection can come from perfection. In the same way, perfect joy arises from perfect joy." We cannot wait for a time when something on the outside might provide supreme joy, peace, or love . . . we would wait forever. We should not attempt to get to the sublime by way of externals. Rather, the Siddha tradition teaches that we must go inward and seek it directly from the divine core of our being.

Gurumayi is speaking about something beyond "ordinary" joy, peace, and love; she is referring to the *para* form of these terms, indicating the highest, most subtle, the transcendent: *paramānanda*, supreme bliss, *paramaśāntiḥ*, supreme peace, *parābhakti*, divine love. "The joy that we are talking about," she says, "is an inner state. It is the *antarāvasthā*, the state of one's own elevated mind and purified heart. It is not just a certain feeling or a giddy emotion. . . ."

So beautiful, so lofty a concept: to experience divine love at its source. But how can this actually be accomplished? Gurumayi teaches, as does the philosophy of Kashmir Shaivism, that the answer is in the quality of daily living, in daily attitudes and disciplines: The purpose of *sādhana* is that we live better in the world, that we improve the quality of our own lives and in turn the lives of those around us. Therefore, such practices as chanting, meditation, contemplation, and prayer, as well as maintaining vigilant awareness of our utterances and conduct, serve to purify and strengthen our entire being.

Sādhana is spiritual discipline. It is a collection of the formal practices that provide a means to the goal, while allowing us to participate in glimpses of the goal along the way. The conscious nurturing of contentment, for example, is such a practice. Says Gurumayi, "Contentment saves you from everything that exhausts you and defeats you and wastes your energy. It acts like soothing ointment on a nervous system ridden by anxieties. By practicing contentment, you are able to live life as it should be. . . ."

It is through these practices that the devotee can begin to make real spiritual progress toward the experience of supreme love, and to become firmly established in that experience. The Siddha tradition maintains that we cannot change just by wishing it; we must strengthen ourselves with the practices. The purpose of the practices is not to attract the grace of God, but to become a strong enough vessel to contain and be cognizant of the grace that is already there. Of course, in a very advanced spiritual state, the highest perception — the complete immersion in and identification with that grace — can be induced at will. In Kashmir Shaiva philosophy this is called the *icchā upāya* ("path of will"), where divine consciousness can be entered into just by the thought of it, just by willing it to be so. However, a *sādhaka* who has arrived at *icchā upāya* must first have mastered the will in an ordinary sense, and such mastery is developed through the practices. Without the support of the practices, we might jump right into *sādhana* and announce to ourselves: "Today things will go differently. My outlook will change, my actions and reactions will change."

But if we are working with the sole support of a limited, contracted, worldly starting point, then worldly, exterior interference is certain to undermine our best intentions.

Once true joy, peace, and love — the *para*, the sublime, the divine joy, peace, and love — are uncovered, however, the world becomes transformed for us, according to our vision, our needs, our own situation. Then, no crisis can be too trying. Right in the thick of an especially difficult situation, we will be buoyed up; we may even be able to watch it as a drama unfolding, and still feel joy bubbling up from within, for the source of deep and serene joy is not in any external situation, but in the ever-continuous consciousness of God. This is why Gurumayi reminds us, as did her spiritual predecessors, to go directly within to the source of that joy and peace and love. Then the power of that divinity will filter into the situations of ordinary life. This is what Utpaladeva was talking about when he glorified those who are completely immersed in divine love:

> For them, this turbulent ocean of the world
> Is like a great pleasure-lake
> For their amusement. [*Śivastotrāvalī* 3.15]

It is from this state that Gurumayi speaks when she talks about supreme joy, specifically the joy of giving: "It is your own heart soaked in God's abundance which is streaming into the universe." At this point in her talk, she breaks into an intoxicating *abhanga* (verse) of the Maharashtrian poet-saint Tukaram Maharaj:

> In the great flood of bliss,
> Waves are surging, and they too are nothing but bliss,
> For bliss is the nature of every particle
>   of this body of bliss.

On one evening, so abundant was Gurumayi's joy in sharing the magnificent verses of the poet-saints that she invited everyone to sing along with her in celebrating the ecstatic expression of the Sufi saint Mansur Mastana. In those moments, we were given an impromptu lesson in the pronunciation of the original language, a mixture of medieval Persian and Hindustani, and as we joined in, accompanied by the harmonium, we became swept up into the intoxicating melody. It was as if a window into that divine, abundant, supreme consciousness had been graciously opened, and we were being invited to the other side and bestowed a sumptuous experience of that sublime, transcendent *para* state of perfect joy-love-peace.

But then, after such intoxicating interludes, lest we feel that we ourselves could never again bridge the gap between two types of existence, that the scriptures and the *siddhas* belong to one realm, while we belong to another, Gurumayi offers assurance. As one example, she refers to the classic situation at the center of the *Bhagavad Gītā*, drawing the scriptures right into practical application. "Arjuna's problem," she points out, "is everyone's problem." Like Arjuna, we might assume that our "spiritual" life is one thing, and our "real" (!) one is another. The *Bhagavad Gītā* addresses these seeming contradictions and teaches that every single one of our actions in life actually constitutes *sādhana*. The celebrated scripture teaches that it is indeed possible—even necessary—to transcend the world while still engaging in ordinary worldly activities and responsibilities. This is accomplished by maintaining a single focus—on God. This does not mean that the world should be neglected. On the contrary, its magnificence should be glorified. But how can a realistic, and graceful, synthesis be achieved?

Experiencing absolute joy, peace, and love amid distractions —whether adverse or enticing—such is true *sādhana*. And yet, the power of contemplative practices helps us to evaluate every situation with newfound authority. Maintaining equanimity in the midst of a storm is not the same as bending and being crushed by it. Gurumayi urges us to consider: "How can you hope to rise to nobility of spirit when you spend your time with a low-minded person who is obsessed with his own degraded goals and values?" *Sādhana* requires constant self-evaluation, constant vigilance. Lives change in unexpected ways as we learn to act in accordance with interior wisdom. How, then, does the devotee know which choices are appropriate, which radical changes are for the best? Again and again comes the answer: Turn within, ask for divine guidance, and never underestimate the power of the practices.

So let us read. Let us imbibe the timeless truths brought to light during one special Christmas week. As we read this book, let us visualize our hearts leaping up in gladness at the good news — that there is yet another chance, that we can refresh and actually prolong our experience of supreme joy, peace, and love — right here, right now.

Constantina Rhodes Bailly

Constantina Rhodes Bailly, Ph.D., is a distinguished scholar of Kashmir Shaivism and the translator of Utpaladeva's Meditations on Shiva: The Śivastotrāvalī, *published by the State University of New York Press. Currently a professor in the Department of Religious Studies at Eckerd College in St. Petersburg, Florida, she is preparing a book on the goddess Lakṣmī. Professor Bailly is also a member of the faculty of the Indological Research Center at Gurudev Siddha Peeth in Ganeshpuri, India.*

INNER TREASURES

INVOCATION

Muktānandāya gurave śhiṣhya-saṃsāra-hāriṇe
Bhakta-kāryaika-dehāya namaste chit-sad-ātmane

Om namaḥ śhivāya gurave sac-chid-ānanda-mūrtaye
Niṣhprapañchāya śhāntāya nirālambāya tejase

Om saha nāvavatu saha nau bhunaktu
Saha vīryam karavāvahai
Tejasvi nāvadhītam astu mā vidviṣhāvahai

Om śhāntiḥ śhāntiḥ śhāntiḥ
Sadgurunāth Mahārāj kī Jaya!

Salutations to Muktananda, the Guru,
who rescues his disciples from the cycle of birth and death,
who has assumed a body to meet the needs of his devotees,
and whose nature is consciousness and being.

Om. Salutations to the Guru, who is Shiva!
His form is being, consciousness, and bliss.
He is transcendent, calm, free from all support, and luminous.

Om. May we, Guru and disciple, be protected together.
May we enjoy the fruits of our actions together.
May we achieve strength together.
May our knowledge be full of light.
May we never have enmity for one another.

Om. Peace. Peace. Peace.
I hail the Master who has revealed the Truth to me!

THE MIRROR
OF GOD

With great respect and great love, I welcome you all with all my heart.

Why is it always so powerful to celebrate the birth of a great being? Even the death of a great being has the same effect. Opening our hearts to honor a great soul, at any time, in any way, arrests our thoughts in the deep stillness of the Himalayas and immerses us in the bottomless pool of God's love. Before we know it, we have become intoxicated with the magnificence of our own soul.

Why does a great being affect us like this? How can you put the experience of their love in words? The *Yoga Vāsiṣṭha* provides a remarkable answer. This text is one of the great works in Indian philosophy on the nature of the mind. In it, the sage Vasishtha says:

anāptākhilaśhailādi pratibimbe hi yādṛiśhī /
syāddarpaṇe darpaṇatā kevalātmasvarūpiṇī // [3:4:57]

The mind of a great being reflects the image of God
    as if it were a mirror.
All other minds are like blocks of stone,
Incapable of reflecting anything at all.

The mind of a great being is so clear and pure, it constantly experiences its own freedom. Its perception is sublime. The light of God floods such a mind. A great being thinks and speaks of nothing but God; all his actions are about pleasing God; and in turn, God flows through him. Or, to put it another way: because the mind of a great being is so finely tuned to God's will, following in his footsteps brings you to God. His mind is bright with the luster of the divine impulse. When he speaks, you know instinctively that you are hearing the truth. His heart is so full of compassion that wherever he goes, the earth sends fresh shoots to cushion his feet. If that isn't possible, then she makes herself softer.

Today is a wonderful day, a very auspicious occasion, the anniversary of the birth of Jesus Christ. It reminds us all that God is not far away, God is within us. On days like this, there is no denying the love that bubbles in everyone's heart. The physical body can hardly contain it. Love floods through the eyes, manifesting God's presence; it flows through the hands, which want to offer selfless service. On Christmas morning, we are so grateful for God's creation that we want to sing His praises with greater fervor. We want to thank Him for everything that He has bestowed upon us.

Tukaram Maharaj, a poet-saint from western India, was a simple man who attained a state of oneness with the Absolute, and became a mirror of the Divine. From his pure mind came thousands of devotional songs, or *abhangas*, about the Lord, His devotees, and the spiritual path. If you ever want to know how to experience the nectar of loving the saints, you can always turn to him. In one of his *abhangas*, Tukaram sang:

sarvapakṣhīṅ hari sāhe sakhā jhālā /
olyā aṅgaṇīṅchyā kalpalatā tyālā //

sahajachālīṅ chālatāṅ pāyavāṭe /
chintāmaṇīsamāna hotā goṭe //

aise haribhaktācheṅ jñāna mahimāna /
atarkya tyācheṅ durlabha darśhana //

When a person is a true friend of God,
Even the plants in his courtyard are wish-fulfilling trees.

As he strolls on his way,
The stones under his feet become wish-fulfilling gems.

The wisdom of such a devotee is exalted.
The *darśhan* of such a being is beyond
   the grasp of the intellect.

"Beyond the grasp of the intellect . . ." This is why, when you see a photograph of a great being or touch something a great being once held in his hand, your heart is flooded with joy and your intellect asks curiously, "What is it? Why do you feel like this? What's happening?"

Another great saint from western India, one who lived in this century, was called Hari Giri Baba. Swami Muktananda, my Guru, loved him very much. Hari Giri Baba had this incredible habit of collecting pebbles as he walked. He would examine each pebble he picked up and say, "This is worth a hundred rupees! This one is worth ten thousand rupees. And this one! This one is worth one million rupees." Then he would put it in his pocket, which was always full of stones. Sometimes, if the seeker was sincere in his devotion, Hari Giri Baba would present him with a small stone, and all his blessings, more precious than gems, were in it.

To this day, people who met Hari Giri Baba still remember his ecstatic laughter. The laughter of an enlightened being is uncanny. It comes from *parāvāṇi*, the highest level of speech, which is pure Consciousness, the source of all sound. The laughter of the saints roars out of that place of absolute silence.

One of the devotees in the little town where Hari Giri Baba spent most of his life once said, "A lot of people here still think he was just an eccentric, crazy old man. But I tell you, by being in his presence, my life was transformed. Everything Hari Giri Baba said, every blessing, every teaching, every glance that I received from him changed me completely.

It is because of him that I am a happy man today. It is because of his grace."

The mind of a great being is free from worldly desires. He wants nothing. Therefore, he no longer lives for himself alone. His one desire is that others might also be free, that others might find their way out of suffering and into joy. It is a rapturous experience to celebrate the life of a great being when you recognize one and are blessed with his teachings. For such beings are very rare, like a plant in the desert that blooms only once every hundred years.

Now what about the lives of those who have not allowed God's grace to transform them?

A mind which has not been purified by God's touch, a mind that remains ignorant, gets tossed around like a ship without a rudder, lost at sea. When the mind has no higher goal to achieve, sooner or later it finds life dull and insipid. It behaves like a scavenger, roaming from place to place, collecting and feeding on dirt and rotting things, never noticing the simple sacred beauty of creation. In the *Yoga Vāsishtha*, the sage Vasishtha says:

śhāśhvatenaikarūpeṇa niśhchayena vinā sthitiḥ /
yena sā chittamityuktā tasmājjātamidaṁ jagat // [3:93:39]

When the mind has no fixed purpose and is unsteady,
Its inner changes reflect the ups and downs
    of the outer world.

Many people think they are fulfilling their purpose in life if they get what they want. If they are able to satisfy a desire or complete a project on schedule, as planned, then their minds are steady. Or so they think. Many people carry this idea to such an extreme, they say things like, "I have everything I want. Why do I need God? Who is God? I am quite happy with my life. What more can God do for me?"

Statements like these are the signposts of an unpurified mind. They are the front gate, the doorbell, the threshold of ignorance. When Vasishtha talks about fixed purpose, he is definitely not talking about desires. He is not talking about a tiger stalking its prey or a lover of sweets gazing at his favorite cake hours before it is time for dessert. The phrase "fixed purpose" does not mean being obsessed by an unsettling interaction you had with somebody or being fixated on a particular seat that you want in the hall. That kind of purposeful intensity is completely misdirected. It is like chewing on the thick skin of a pomegranate and throwing away the juicy red gems inside, or like a child wanting the moon for his birthday gift. Nor does one-pointed focus mean thinking constantly about the one member of your family who wasn't there for Christmas dinner. The sage is not speaking about fixing your purpose on a host of unfulfilled desires or unrealistic expectations, and charging them with all your energy and time.

People do this all the time in their daily lives, don't they? They say, "I've got to have this or that . . . my heart is set on it. . . ." They say, "I made up my mind once and for all. . . ." But that is backwards. What does the sage mean by "fixed purpose"? He means fixing the mind on a higher truth, on God's love. When Vasishtha speaks about unsteadiness, he is referring to a mind that has not tasted the nectar of the divine Presence, a crude mind which has not been disciplined by yoga or purified in the wisdom of the soul. He means that you have not fallen in love with God or experienced His compassion. Such a mind tends to live in a web of illusions that it has intricately woven out of itself. It can only act and react to the changing tides of *samsāra*, the ocean of appearances. Sooner or later, a mind like that is bound to experience calamity. Then, of course, it flounders and thrashes around in despair. Such a mind is very susceptible to dark feelings. It is always whining.

The mind of a great being has been burned in the fire of spiritual practice. It has totally surrendered itself to the will of God. Therefore, such a mind is free from selfishness and the attachment to worldly life. It is utterly pure and at rest in the temple of the heart, where the Supreme Lord dwells in His fullness.

The renowned Sufi Master Jalaluddin Rumi glorifies the great beings and defines their state quite accurately in these lines:

> You may see holy ones down with you on earth,
> But their place is actually higher than the skies.
> Someone may appear to be living in the world,
> Whose spirit resides in the seventh heaven.

Do you see what Rumi means? He is deciphering a sacred mystery for you. He is saying that when you give your adoration to a great being, what you are really celebrating is your own higher Self, your own greater Consciousness. When you give your love to an exalted one, you feel so uplifted that at least for a few brief moments, you are in the seventh heaven; you are living in the *sahasrāra*, the highest spiritual center in the crown of the head, with the awareness of *So'ham:* "I am That. I am That. I am one with God."

Out of their love for the people of this earth, the great beings take form and live among us. If you catch even a tiny glimpse of how much love they have for people, for animals, birds, and everything that is worthy of love, then your heart soars in delight. You are filled with conviction. You know that by being in their presence and following their teachings, you are walking the right path. It feels so dharmic, so righteous, doesn't it? To inhale the fragrance of the teachings of the Masters, to be embraced by their wisdom, to receive their blessings, to have the courage to discover a new day every morning.

These teachings are the real nourishment of life. Even if years and centuries go by, even if natural calamities change the face of the planet, the teachings of the great beings spring forth anew. Or, from time to time, they are unearthed — old treasures perhaps, but still alive with Consciousness, still essential. Such teachings are never destroyed; nor does the subtle presence of such divine beings ever diminish. This is something quite reassuring to keep in mind: that which is truly precious can never be extinguished.

In the Indian scriptures, it is said that a great being roams in the space of Consciousness, *chidākāśha*. Although his body may appear to be made of flesh and bones like any other human being, his true dwelling is in the light of God.

A Sufi saint unveils his vision of the Master in this song:

tū pastime, ālāme, aur rūbarū hai /
banā tū har eka phūla meṅ raṅga aur bū hai //

aur āīnā dekhā, to tū rūbarū hai /
nigāha jisa tarapha uṭha gaī tū hī tū hai //

magara rāza ika aur, aba yaha khulā hai /
ki maiṅ tujhameṅ, aur mujhameṅ tū basa rahā hai //

You are in the lowest depths and the highest skies,
And You are ever-present.
You have become the fragrance
And the glistening color in every flower.

When I looked in the mirror,
I found myself face to face with You.
Wherever my glance fell I saw You.

But one secret has now become apparent.
That I am in You, and You are living in me.

"When I looked in the mirror, I found myself face to face with You." What mirror does he mean? The mirror of the heart.

To make real progress in one's spiritual practices, the grace of a great being is vital. Just as someone who has traversed a path can guide others along that same way, similarly, a great being who has become completely established in the awareness of God can also impart that profound experience to others. Those who say that they can reach the goal on their own, without divine guidance or the intervention of grace, are like a rock that says, "In time I will become a beautiful statue. No sculptor needs to work on me."

So far, no such thing has ever happened. There may be some dramatically beautiful rock formations in this world, created by constant rainfall, by waves crashing on the seashore, by centuries of erosion. But they are not like the statues that are fashioned by the hand of a master, by one who can sculpt the vision of a sage or translate into stone the images that rise from the depths of his own creativity. Only a master can transform an ordinary rock into a magnificent *mūrti*, an image worthy of worship in a temple.

The *Paramārthasāra* is one of the central texts of the profound spiritual tradition known as Kashmir Shaivism. In one of its verses, the tenth-century Siddha Guru Abhinavagupta says:

ādarśhe malarahite yadvad vadanam vibhāti tadvadayam /
śhiva-śhaktipātavimale dhītattve bhāti bhāvarūpaḥ //

Just as a face clearly appears in a spotless mirror,
In the same way, the Self shines in all its splendor
In the intellect that has been purified by Shiva's *śhaktipāt*.

In the initiation known as Shiva's *śhaktipāt*, the transmission of divine energy occurs through the grace of a great being. Once awakened, this energy purifies the mind and the intellect, so that they can reflect the radiance of the divine Presence. Over and over again, all the scriptures speak about the cleansing of the mind, the body, and the soul. This purification is intense. It is not just a question of having a few good thoughts here and there. Purification does not begin and end with physical fitness, either. Even the body that you think is quite healthy can only take you so far. The body is going to fall away, sooner or later. Only the soul lives on.

Nor, when we speak about the Supreme Self shining in all its splendor, are we speaking about the soul glorifying the

Lord every now and then. The doctrine of purification is quite rigorous and thorough. It is a process that is not complete until one's own limited self has been utterly annihilated. Freedom from the ego is a state of unbounded ecstasy, that is true. However, the process that one must undergo to attain this freedom can be quite agonizing. Even so, the reward cannot be surpassed.

It seems very comfortable to think of God's love in the form of a gentle breeze, a sweet whisper in the night, or some divine rescue during difficult times. Nevertheless, truly speaking, when very deep purification is taking place, God's love acts like a great fire, ruthlessly burning your limitations away.

My Guru, Baba Muktananda, vibrated with kindness and compassion. A woman who had never heard of Baba or of Siddha Yoga happened to come upon a photograph of him. She stopped what she was doing and picked up the picture. She gazed at it intently for a moment. Then she looked up and said, "What a kind man. His compassion must be incredible!"

Although Baba's love was as cooling as moonbeams and sweeter than you could ever anticipate, he also manifested every color of the blazing fire of God. In his book *The Perfect Relationship*, he says, "There is something that you should remember: A person who becomes aware of his own ignorance is drawn to the Guru's feet. But the pride of knowledge gleaned from dry books leads one to look for scriptures, rather than for a Guru. Although the scriptures emphasize surrender, vows, and discipline, they are lifeless. So one does not really have to surrender to them. One can interpret them in any way one likes. But, one cannot interpret the Guru.

"You can change the scriptures, but the Guru will certainly change you. He will begin by awakening you, by telling you that you have forgotten your Self. Lacking knowledge of your Self, you are deep in the sleep of ignorance. The Guru will open your eyes to your darkness, ignorance, and forgetfulness.

"Only after knowing darkness is it possible to find light. Only one who falls can get up. Unless a seeker knows what it is to fall down, it is difficult for him to rise. After the Guru has made you aware of your condition, he will give you the vision of your own Self."

This is what we celebrate at Christmas—the birth of one who carried the divine torch so radiantly within him that other souls, for hundreds and thousands of years, caught fire from his flame, found the Supreme Lord in his teachings, and became one with the peace, joy, and love that reign in the world within the heart.

And so we all say, "Merry Christmas." With great respect and great love, I welcome you all with all my heart.

December 25, 1994

Chapter One

THE SADHANA
OF JOY

With great respect and great love, I welcome you all with all my heart.

We are on the threshold of a new year. Joy, peace, and love are ringing in the air. Most people attribute this delightful condition to the Christmas spirit, and it is true, during Christmas week people seem to be more joyous, more peaceful, and more loving. Or at least you might say they make an attempt to be joyful, peaceful, and loving. Somehow people have gotten the idea that these experiences are more available at this time of year.

In reality, joy, peace, and love are the very nature of your own inner Self. They are not seasonal. They are the birthright, the inheritance, and the essence of every living being.

So, tonight we are going to investigate joy. True joy is something that is easier to share than to articulate. Still, we are going to make a conscious effort to inquire into the matter and see how it applies to each one of us. We are going to trace joy back to its source. And if, along the way, we happen to find ourselves rejoicing. . . . Well, that is one of the basic characteristics of joy — the moment you uncover it, it starts to spread. It can even transform our perception of the world.

In the *Atharva Veda*, one of the most ancient Indian scriptures, the sages invoke the power of joy, saying:

śhanno vāto vāyu śhannastapatu sūryaḥ /
ahāni śham bhavantu naḥ śham rātrī prati dhīyatām /
śham uṣhā no vyucchatu // [7:69]

May the wind blow us joy.
May the sun shine down joy on us.
May our days pass with joy.
May the night be a gift of joyful peace!
May the dawn bring us joy at its coming!

This prayer is exquisite. It presents us with a vision of the universe as entirely alive, pregnant with joy. It understands that each element, each aspect of this world has the power to bestow happiness. It addresses each one with gentleness and humility. You can almost feel the sweet apprehension with which the sages entreat the forces of the universe, and you can also feel their joy. It is with joy that the sages invoke the power of joy. So, their joy is echoed and multiplied a thousand times.

Welcoming the wind, the sunshine, the days, the nights, every moment, every person, every object, every task, with all the joy in your own heart and also knowing, beyond a shadow of a doubt, that joy is what you will receive from them—in this way, you create a palace of joy to live in. You surround yourself with joy—within and without, above and below. You give joy; you see joy; you breathe joy. And then, when you see someone, your mind says to you, "What a joy it is to see Luke! What a joy Chandrika is! I really like talking to John these days. I just love being with them." You are able to carry this lighthearted feeling to everyone you meet, and to each element of the universe. Even when you drink a glass of water, you think, "Oh, I never knew water could taste so good! Isn't it delightful?"

Whether you believe in God or not, each one of you has a basic desire for happiness. When that desire is frustrated, it is very common for you to feel jealous of someone else's joy—jealous and a little baffled. "What has she got to be so happy about?" Have you ever heard that? Have you ever thought it? If you are not happy, you simply cannot understand how anyone else can be; and so you look for flaws in them or in their situation. But the fact is, unless you realize the value of human life itself, and the transcendent joy that is woven through all of creation, you will never know what real happiness is.

My Guru, Baba Muktananda, had merged his awareness into this vision of the universe and there was no end to his joy and his love. Baba always repeated, "Know your own Self. Follow the dharma, the duties, of your own life and find God there." It is the plain truth. Joy comes to those who apply themselves to their daily duties, and experience the presence of the great Self within and without.

Yesterday I met with a devotee who has been taking care of her handicapped child for the last year and a half. When I saw her, she was so filled with light, joy, peace, and love. I was very pleased and my heart was moved, knowing all the suffering she has gone through for so many months. She has become more beautiful, inside and out. Her contentment is so deep; her faith in God is so strong. She had applied herself generously to her daily duties—it didn't matter what they were—and she is drinking the nectar of God's love.

So, you see, we are not talking about the so-called conventional joys, the kind that come from a little bit of praise here and there, a few accomplishments, a few gifts, a few good meals, a few attachments—or the joy that you derive from comparing yourself to others and coming out on top, the joy of vanity appeased or competitions won. Nor are we referring to the kind of joy that crops up now and then on the spiritual path, the joy of thinking of yourself as someone very evolved, while your poor friends struggle on in darkness.

Joys such as these are very short-lived. They don't have much substance. Their foundation is flimsy. And since they do not have a strong transcendent quality, they cannot infuse you with the strength or purity you need for liberation.

A modern Indian scholar has very clearly explained the distinction between mundane joy and divine joy. He said, "The worms that only live in the bitter neem fruit seem tortured when placed in sugar. In the same way, the ignorant one who seeks the pleasures of the world of duality fears the joy of the nondual, of the unmanifest, since he can find there no trace of the songs and dance and play of this world. Yet those who attain knowledge realize that it is only beyond duality that the essence of true joy can be found. Thus, Rudra [the fierce aspect of God], who is feared by the ignorant, appears to the wise as the auspicious Shiva [the transcendent One], the ambrosia of all joy."

It is hard to recognize spiritual joy when all your past experience has come through the senses, from the excitement of a desire fulfilled. This is what the Indian scriptures refer to as ignorance. A person in this predicament is often afraid of God, because he is unsure of God's compassion, of God's way of doing things. Therefore, he imposes his own dark feelings onto God and never tastes the joy of the Self. However, the knowers of the Truth, those of wise and steady minds, see God as the embodiment of auspiciousness and the ambrosia of all joy.

When you don't know God's ways, you suffer. Even to experience joy, one must do the *sādhana* of joy. Joy is a spiritual practice. It is also the fruit of spiritual practice. That is to say, the ecstasy that the poet-saint Tukaram Maharaj expressed is always within your grasp, even while you are walking the path. Listen to the way Tukaram Maharaj described this state:

ānandāche dohiṅ ānanda taranga /
ānandachi anga ānandāchem //

In the great flood of bliss,
Waves are surging, and they too are nothing but bliss,
For bliss is the nature of every particle
   of this body of bliss.

All week long, people have been sending waves and waves of joy my way. It has been an amazing experience. When I first returned from India, the people here expressed incredible joy. A few days passed and they settled back into their daily life. Then more people came and they brought waves of fresh joy with them. And then, they too settled into the daily routine of the ashram. Then, once again, a few more people came and they brought this really wonderfully fresh joy with them. So, all this time, you have been settling in and I have been experiencing waves and waves and waves of joy. Sometimes I wonder if my cheeks can survive all the smiling.

Right now, with the help of the Christmas spirit, you are all doing the *sādhana* of joy. You are making an effort to discover the key to joy. You are like explorers in pursuit of the secret passage into the ocean of joy. There may be a little fear of the unknown in you. Still, by giving yourself to the practice and the discipline of joy, you have stepped into a circle of protection formed by grace, and everything will come to you in time. Besides, as an English writer once said, "If you go to heaven without being naturally qualified for it, you will not enjoy yourself there."

The *sādhana* of joy has its own value. It is its own reward. If you don't know what you are striving for, or what your heart truly wants, then even if you attain the best of all things, even if you are handed the immortal fruit, even if you are planted in paradise, you will be as confused as ever. And you'll miss out on the time of your life.

Joy is great and it is great to experience joy. But you must also know that *you* are great. Never forget that. It is where true joy lies — in the secret of your greatness, in the Self that makes you great. My Guru, Baba Muktananda, was always immersed in bliss. It flowed from his fingers. It crackled in his laugh. In *Mukteshwari*, one of his books of aphorisms, Baba said:

> There is perfect joy within the heart,
> a love like nectar —
> Go there and find it.

Isn't it interesting? Most people in this modern world are willing to indulge in all the faults and vices that exist within them. Yet they are reluctant to admit that they are also the temple of virtue and joy. Why are they so resistant to their own greatness? Virtue and joy exist inside each one. The sages never stop pointing this out. "Turn within," they say again and again, "That's where you've got everything. Look inside." They also keep telling you that you actually have the power to hold on to what is good for you and renounce what is harmful. Isn't it a great wonder! That much freedom, that much authority is given to each human being.

Baba said, joy is constantly bubbling up in your heart. Not only was this Baba's experience, he also unlocked this experience in thousands of hearts. Perfect joy. Joy without dependency. Joy that is whole. Joy that is everlasting. Joy that never decays. Joy that is free from likes and dislikes. Joy that places itself in the service of God, that never leaves His presence for a second. Joy that is contagious, that is giving. Such perfect joy really does exist in everyone's heart.

The sages faithfully remind us to sustain the awareness, "I am perfect, I am pure." Baba imparted the same teachings to all of us. So many times during his talks and meditation instructions he asked seekers to cultivate this awareness, "I am perfect, I am pure, I am bliss, I am love."

When you are not feeling good about yourself, not experiencing a great state in your meditations, you may resist this teaching. You may be reluctant to contemplate it and you can't imagine putting it into practice. I remember an Intensive that Baba gave in Miami in 1980. He had just given a wonderful talk on Lord Shiva as the inner presence in each human being, the deepest, lightest, most vibrant part of us. Then, when meditation began, he showed us how to imbibe this teaching. "Have this awareness," Baba kept saying. "Repeat it to yourself: 'I am Shiva. I am perfect. I am pure. I am love.'" He was saying it with so much authority, with so much power, so much freedom, so much conviction.

Now, on that particular day, I wasn't exactly in a sensational state. So every time Baba said, "Have this awareness — 'I am Shiva and I am pure,'" I kept telling myself, "No. I'm not." I thought, "That's not what I feel and I won't fake it."

Baba's voice kept booming, "Have this awareness: 'I am Shiva. I am love.'" And I kept thinking, "Oh no. Not again. Can't he understand? Everyone's heard him. Everyone's got it. I don't want to hear it again."

That day, it seemed, he just couldn't stop. He kept saying it and saying it, over and over. And I kept feeling more and more horrible, "See. . . I knew it. That's not for me. . . at least not today."

Finally, after what seemed like eons, I suddenly found myself hearing the same words being spoken inside me, "I am Shiva." The words started to ring inside me, and yet they were also beyond me — beyond my mind, beyond my state. They grew stronger and stronger, resonating through my entire being. "I am the Self. I am perfect. I am love. I am Shiva." Hearing this, I went into deep meditation.

Only perfection can come from perfection. In the same way, perfect joy arises from perfect joy. When you experience your own great Self, which is taintless, which is immutable, unborn, spacious, higher than the highest, subtler than the subtlest, it happens.

With this experience comes the understanding of joy. You realize that it abides in your own being. It is part of you.

Actually, it *is* you. In fact, rays of pure joy are continually emanating from you and from all beings. They vibrate in the universe. They shimmer.

Perfect joy is so independent, so free, that it wells up for no reason at all. Your mind and intellect cannot comprehend it. But when it comes, it spills into everything you do. You find yourself singing for the sheer joy of it. You find joy in completing a task that needs your attention. You find joy in sitting quietly by yourself. Worship gives you joy. Your heart beats with joy. You can almost feel every cell in your body pulsating with gladness.

Now allow me to tell you what perfect joy is not. It is not the same thing as laughing at other people's mistakes. It never secretly gloats over another person's shortcomings or makes a joke at someone else's expense. It doesn't sit in a corner and fret. It can't be attained by amassing wealth and possessions. It won't come into your fold if you run after it. It simply cannot stay where people and all the things of this world aren't rightly respected. Perfect joy is not the by-product of a business transaction, either. It isn't half-happy and half-doubtful. It definitely is not shallow. It isn't a quick smile arising from a sense of duty or courtesy. It doesn't come to those who cannot or will not harbor a few good thoughts.

Perfect joy lives far, far away from disharmony. It is like the sun; it shines on everyone. It just is. If there are storms, if the sky is overcast, thick with clouds, you may not be able to see it. But that does not mean the sun no longer exists. In the same way, you cannot make the joy of the Self happier by dressing it up or unhappy by ignoring it. *Nirantara ānanda rasa svarūpam*, says Shri Shankaracharya, the great sage and Siddha of eighth-century India, in his text *Vivekachūḍāmaṇi* (*The Crest Jewel of Discrimination*): "Supreme Reality is of the nature of unwavering, imperishable joy." The nature of the Self is *ānanda rasa*, the elixir of bliss. It is *nirantara*, uninterrupted.

What is the best means of attaining the experience of unending joy? What can one do to evoke it? There are many answers to that question, many means of attaining joy. Tonight we will take up a few of them, so we can at least scratch the surface of this profound subject, the *sādhana* of joy.

In his book *Reflections of the Self*, Baba Muktananda said:

Be free of all craving,
And joy will be yours.

This is the fundamental teaching of all religious traditions, scriptures, Eastern philosophies, and mystics. It is the common understanding of all those who have experienced the presence of God both in their own hearts and in the universe.

As long as there is any amount of desire, big or small, repressed or uncontrolled, your joy will not endure. Sooner or later it is bound to be eaten up. The problem with desires is that they are so voracious, they grow out of all proportion. If they are not kept in check, they begin to dominate you completely. Then, although you may think you are still in control of your life, you are actually being driven by your desires.

Even so, most people defend their desires, tooth and nail. They fight for the right to fulfill them. But then, they should also expect to spend a lot of time in the depths of depression. Depression is the rent you pay for living in desire. Or, to put it another way, if you plant a desire and give it plenty of nourishment, don't expect to harvest fulfillment. Depression is the fruit you'll reap. And don't feel sorry for yourself, either. You did it. That's what you asked for. There is no one else to blame.

Even if there seems to be a glimmer of joy when a certain desire is satisfied, it will soon be stifled by another desire. Craving darkens the heart. It blocks the natural unfolding of joy. It can't be said enough: freedom from craving is the road to delight.

During the holidays, you are all so joyous. You are. You

can almost see radiant hearts dancing in the air. With so much joy around, of course you can hear celestial music and become intoxicated by the divine Presence. And why are you so loving and so joyous during this time? Because your heart is free from "I want this or that for myself." Instead, you are thinking about what you can do for somebody else. "What gift would my friend like? What sweetness can I bring to somebody who is sick? What goodies should I make for my relatives? How much can I give in charity?" Simply put, it is goodness that you are contemplating, goodness that you are offering; it is the best of yourself. It is more than that, it is your own heart soaked in God's abundance which is streaming into the universe. And so, like Tukaram Maharaj, you can sing:

> In the great flood of bliss,
> Waves are surging, and they too are nothing but bliss,
> For bliss is the very nature of every particle
>   of this body of bliss.

Once a seeker went up to Baba and said, "I am very unhappy, I am just so sad. Can you do something for me, Baba?"

Baba looked at him, and then he asked, "Have you done something kind for anyone today?"

The man looked at Baba in confusion. It was clear he thought Baba did not understand the extent and intensity of his suffering. So he asked the question again, a little louder, to be sure that Baba got the point.

Without hesitating, Baba restated his answer, "Have you done something kind for anyone today?" The man just shook his head and walked away. He had come with a bag loaded with dissatisfaction, and instead of emptying it before the Guru and filling it with the Guru's blissful command, he simply walked away with his bag still heavy, loaded with one more thing to be dissatisfied about. What to do?

Well, whether that man got the message or not, Baba gave

us all a very important teaching that day: If you can do something kind, something caring, something beneficial for someone else, it will always bring you joy then and there. It doesn't really matter whether your lovely action takes much time, or whether it is big or small. If you will do it with a joyful heart, your own suffering will be relegated to the back burner — the energy just goes out of it. It begins to disappear, and there is room for something else to surface. The moment you drop your disappointments, what is left? Your joy, your delight, your bliss.

Do you remember the story that Baba used to tell about the man who was cooking in his imagination? Let me tell it to you again. It is a story that I think about a lot. Events have a way of bringing it to mind.

Once upon a time, there was a man who had been traveling for a long, long way. He was far from home, and well before he reached his destination, he ran completely out of money. One day he had to go without food. The next day he couldn't find anything to eat either. A third day went by. No food. The poor man went without eating for ten days in a row. By this time, he was being tormented by hunger.

Finally, he decided that he had to do something. He couldn't take another step. So, he found a shady tree and he sat down under it. Closing his eyes, he imagined a perfect kitchen in every detail. Then, mentally, he began to prepare a meal fit for a king. He started with the chutney, delicious spicy chutney. But as he cooked — in his imagination, of course — he lost track of how much cayenne pepper he had put in. He loved pepper in his chutney, so, to be on the safe side, he added some more.

He couldn't wait to taste it! He took a bite and — oh! his whole mouth began to burn. His tongue, his cheeks — it was horrible! He must have put twice as much pepper in as he should have. Oh! His poor throat, his tongue, the roof of his mouth! It was agony!

Now, while the traveler was sitting there, another man came along the same road and sat under a neighboring tree. Innocently, this stranger witnessed the whole drama. He was quite fascinated. At first, he thought the man was a lunatic, sitting there with his eyes closed, making all sorts of odd gestures and singing to himself. But then, he realized the fellow was having a hard time. Tears were rolling down his cheeks, his nose was running, he was using his sleeve to wipe his mouth and gasping for breath.

So the stranger went over to him and said, "Pardon me, friend, do you need any help?"

The traveler's eyes popped open. "Water! Water!" he gasped.

The other man got him some water to drink and a wet cloth for his face, and eventually the traveler calmed down enough to tell him what had happened. "Listen, brother, I was wild with hunger," he began.

The other man listened carefully to the whole story, and then he said, "If you had to cook in your imagination, why didn't you make something sweet? You could have cooked anything. You could have made something to soothe your tongue and your throat, your mind and your heart. What a fool you are."

Have you ever done this? Have you ever cooked in your imagination? What kinds of dishes does your mind create? Do they hurt? Do they flood your heart with bliss? And if they do not, why not? The poet-saint of Dehu, Tukaram Maharaj, immersed in God, says that bliss is the nature of reality. Tukaram says:

> In the great flood of bliss,
> Waves are surging, and they too are nothing but bliss,
> For bliss is the very nature of every particle
>   of this body of bliss.

We have looked at the value of being free from cravings as the first step in the *sādhana* of joy. How else can you shake hands with joyfulness? What is another way to remove the clutter that has buried your joyful heart?

An ancient Chinese proverb says, "Keep a green tree in your heart, and perhaps the singing bird will come." What a gorgeous image! Just to know that by keeping your heart young and strong, it will attract the heavenly bird. A good attitude, this proverb is saying, opens the door to a world of joy.

So much of what happens in your life depends on the attitude you adopt in any given situation. If you have a good attitude, then you float. If you have a bad attitude, you drown. It is as simple as that. One of the worst obstacles people encounter, both in *sādhana* and in life, lies in their own attitude. Yet, people with a negative attitude can never accept that about themselves. They always think that they have the best attitude in the world, that the problem is something external, and usually, they want somebody else to fix it.

These are the people who spread anxiety, nervousness, and bitterness wherever they go. But they will never believe that the problem is their own low opinion of the world, their own anger, defensiveness, and so on. Even if you hold a mirror before them, they will still object and try to turn you into the problem—for interfering. Just one more "external" thing to suffer over. They refuse to see that other people are only trying to help them take off the dark and painful blinders they wear, the ones that shut out a loving heart. Truly speaking, it doesn't matter how you treat people who are like this. They are determined to hold their ground. They are right and you are wrong. And so, trying to tell them about developing a good attitude is almost futile.

Ironically, the only people who listen, who can hear you, are the people who already have a good attitude. In fact, listening is one of the signs of a good attitude. It seems a little redundant, telling good people how to become good. Those who are set in their negative ways are always going to think the lesson is for everyone but them.

Nevertheless, by developing a positive attitude toward your own *sādhana* and the things that happen in your life, you will experience a wonderful delight—God's grace, the compassion of Kundalini Shakti, a joy far beyond pleasure and pain. And then, if other people insist on clinging to a negative frame of mind, you can always hope that a time will come in their lives when their defenses are down and the teachings can break through. Perhaps, one morning they will wake up and say, "What a beautiful day! There are such wonderful people in this world! I am so blessed! I am the child of God. Oh, I am so happy today!"

The joy that we are talking about is an inner state. It is the *antarāvasthā*, the state of one's own elevated mind and purified heart. It is not just a certain feeling or a giddy emotion; it is the way you conduct yourself in the privacy of your own being. Joy is the natural state of the Self. It is constant and it can be experienced. Then, just as the space inside a pot and the space outside it are one and the same, similarly, joy is within and joy is without.

Now we have looked into the first two steps in the *sādhana* of joy. First, in Baba's words, "Be free from all craving, and joy will be yours." Secondly, develop a positive attitude. What other ways can we cultivate joy?

The *Vijñāna Bhairava* is one of the principal scriptures of Kashmir Shaivism. It contains 112 *dhāranās*, or centering techniques, which the sages of Kashmir practiced to evoke the experience of the ever-blissful Self. One of these *dhāranās* gives us a divine hint about attaining this joy or even intensifying it. The *Vijñāna Bhairava* says:

yatra yatra manastuṣhtirmanastatraiva dhārayet /
tatra tatra parānandasvarūpam sampravartate // [74]

Wherever a person's mind finds deep joy,
Let it focus on that.

In every such case, the true nature of the highest bliss
will manifest.

This is such a simple and far-reaching technique. It is
something you can practice at any time of the day or night.
Holding on to the state of joy is one of the hardest things to
do. That is why this is such a great exercise.

Throughout your day, watch carefully for any moment
when your mind abandons itself to happiness. Learn to seize
that experience and sustain the feeling for as long as you can.
Focus on it attentively. Don't feel guilty about spending your
time focusing on this feeling which seems to have come out
of nowhere. Don't feel that you are not worthy of it. Do not
entertain, not even for a moment, the idea that this couldn't
be happening to you. Just fix your mind on the sweet joy you
are experiencing.

If you perform this *dhāraṇā*, this centering technique,
often, with one-pointed determination, it is just a matter of
time before you tap into bliss. The highest bliss springs from
your own simple joy. They come from the same source.

Do you remember all the times you allowed your mind to
be affected by other people's remarks and opinions? You let your
attention become absorbed in their harsh words and it totally
tore you up inside. Well, this *dhāraṇā* works in exactly the
same way. It is just the other side of the coin. By focusing
attentively on your own self-born joy, you open the gate to
the kingdom of God. When you become strong in this awareness, then you can truly say, "God is love. God is bliss. The
universe is filled with wondrous joy. The gift of joy is my
greatest attainment. My own inner Self is of the nature of
unending joy." *Nirantara ānanda rasa svarūpam.*

There was once a doctor, a very learned man, who had a
great yearning for the Truth. For years he had been praying to
meet a true teacher, a *sadguru.*

One evening when he knelt in prayer, an inner voice told

him to get up and go outside and be quick about it or he would miss the one he was looking for. The doctor practically ran out of his home. But the only person in sight was a beggar in tattered clothing and worn-out shoes. As the doctor approached, he saw the man had eyes of fire. The doctor was a little taken aback. Almost timidly, he said, "Good day."

"I never had a bad one," said the beggar.

"May God grant you good fortune," said the doctor.

And the beggar replied, "I have never had anything else."

"Then may Heaven bless you."

"I am very blessed," said the beggar.

"Who are you, then?"

"A king."

"King of what?"

"My kingdom is my soul. And all that I am, body or being, pays homage to it. For that is a kingdom greater than any on earth."

The doctor asked, "How did you reach this state of perfection?"

"I silenced my five senses and looked within. I could find no rest short of God. And so He revealed Himself to me. Now, I belong to Him, and He belongs to me. Is there any kingdom to compare with mine?"

For this reason as well, Tukaram Maharaj sang:

In the great flood of bliss,
Waves are surging, and they too are nothing but bliss,
For bliss is the nature of every particle
    of this body of bliss.

The deep and lasting joy that the *Vijñāna Bhairava* is referring to has another name—contentment. Whenever contentment settles in your heart, you begin to see the entire universe from a sublime perspective. Therefore, every time you experience even a drop of contentment, hold on to it. Settle into that feeling, that sensation. Focus your entire attention on it for as long as possible, so that it can sink its roots deeper into your consciousness. Contentment is the sign and symbol of true happiness, true joy. It has nothing to do with complacency. This is a very important distinction to understand. Many people misconstrue contentment; they take it for idleness, complacency, or a kind of lazy, dim-witted satisfaction with the status quo.

Genuine contentment does not imply inactivity. Far from it. You continue to act. But in the midst of your activity, you allow yourself to become aware of a state of well-being. Then, you maintain and increase that awareness. It helps you live. The more finely attuned to it you become, the more alert you are to the things that increase your contentment and also to the ones that place it in jeopardy. You begin to protect your happiness. You begin to protect your joy.

For example, when you are eating a meal, you reach a point where the stomach tells you it is satisfied, the point of satiation. If you continue to eat, the body panics. It can't digest the excess food, which in turn ferments inside you and precipitates small colds, infections, and all sorts of chronic ailments. You must learn to listen to your stomach, recognize when it has reached that point of contentment, and never go beyond it.

Now every action, and every interaction, contains this same point, fullness without excess. So, if you apply this principle to every area of your life, if you learn to detect the tender shoots of contentment and help them grow, your joy will become strong and lasting.

There is no exact equivalent in the English language for the Sanskrit words *tuṣhṭi* or *tṛipti* or *santoṣha*. The word *contentment* is as close as we can come, but it really doesn't have the subtlety or range of experience that the sages are referring to. You can't do justice to the greatness of this attainment by merely saying, "Become established in contentment."

For this reason, it is worth taking a closer look at the

meaning of *complacency*. Perhaps, when you come to understand what contentment is not, you will be able to understand what it is. This method is like the phrase employed by Vedantins, those who practice the philosophy of Vedanta. In order to understand the nature of Absolute Reality, they scrutinize everything, saying, *neti neti,* "not this, not this." Then whatever is left is "That," is the Absolute, is God.

One of the standard definitions of *complacent,* according to the dictionary, is "smug": "It may suggest a gloating superiority or a blameworthy lassitude and lack of drive . . . Smug indicates accustomed feelings about oneself of superiority, rectitude, or utter security." Then it cites an example by a modern author, who speaks of "our smug conviction that somehow we are more virtuous than the rest of the world. . . ." The dictionary goes on to say that the words *complacent* and *self-satisfied* "may suggest ill-based pride, self-deception, depreciation of others, indolent or blind inactivity." As you can see, complacency is virtually the opposite of contentment, *santosha*. They do not even come close in meaning.

According to the sacred texts, contentment is a sublime state that arises with the cessation of all desires. There is no way around it; desires belong to the realm of fleeting satisfactions, not lasting happiness.

Over the years, whenever people hear this, they ask the same question. They say, "But if I drop all my desires, how will I live? If I don't have a desire, how can I think? How can I act? How can I feel what I'm feeling?" And they are so *intense* about it, so agitated, so fearful. They really make you feel that if this is the state that desires get you into, renouncing them sounds like a good idea. Truly speaking, if you want to experience the highest bliss, unending and free, then you must get a handle on your desires.

It is a process, a spiritual practice; it is *sādhana*. Every time you are able to renounce a desire, or to become indifferent to it, you add another building block to the temple of your own contentment. You renounce it not because you can't have it, not because it is outside your reach, and not because of sour grapes, either. You give it up, you turn away, because you know a particular desire isn't good for you. So you make a conscious decision. "No. I don't want this." And then you just let it go.

At that very moment, watch the state of your mind. Observe the state of your heart. Pay careful attention to the effects of letting go of something that is bound to lead to disaster, sooner or later.

Unfailingly, every time you are able to unwrap yourself from the lure of desires, you experience an unearthly joy. This response, though very beautiful, is not the same as complete contentment, however. It is like the gleaming dust which is produced when a diamond is being cut and polished. And yet, you know, if you collect all that gleaming dust and press it together, the result is another diamond. Not a thousand-carat diamond in all its resplendence, perhaps, but still one that is made of the same substance. In the same way, even if your experience of contentment is not the state of *santoṣha* in all its pristine grandeur, it is still contentment. You are practicing contentment, step by step, like a student acquiring knowledge steadily, over time, until he qualifies for a degree.

Of course, it requires practice and effort. How else can you reach a worthwhile goal? There's no point in acting like someone who wants to reach the opposite bank of a rushing river without getting wet, without the hardship of swimming, or the bother of finding a bridge or a ferry. A person like this simply wants to blink his eyes and be there, instantly. But no matter how strong his desire may be, he cannot wish himself to the other shore.

People have many misconceptions about contentment. They think, "What will such a person give to the world? Nothing. He's content. . . ." "What good are they? Why should they care about other people? They're content." This is a very common misunderstanding. However, contentment does not lead to inactivity. On the contrary, it is the state that allows every activity to come to fruition. When you perform action from the source of contentment, it has beauty and sanctity. When you act out of anxiety, nervousness, and twenty cups of coffee, then that's what you give to the world.

Contentment saves you from everything that exhausts you, and defeats you, and wastes your energy. It acts like soothing ointment on a nervous system ridden by anxieties. By practicing contentment, you are able to live life as it should be, without being trampled by the six enemies, the emotions such as anger, jealousy, greed, and so on.

Supreme contentment is what an accomplished yogi experiences. He is active when he seems to be inactive. He is inactive when he seems to be active. In simple language, this means that he follows the will of God and not the dictates of the senses. Trying to comprehend such a yogi from a worldly point of view can be very misleading.

The technique that the *Vijñāna Bhairava* offers us is both effective and beautiful—to focus the mind wherever it finds profound joy, taintless joy. Become steadfast in this practice and you will experience the splendor of the Self. Try it. Instead of giving your mind things that are disappointing or frustrating, instead of cooking with hot pepper in your imagination, give your mind things that are uplifting, that are joyful. Give yourself to those actions that really bring joy into your life. Give yourself to those moments that let you reap joy, that bring you delight. Think of your child laughing, or stroking your cheeks. Think of a friend who has been kind to you during difficult times, been loyal and loving, no matter what. Think of the ocean, think of the mountains, think of the sky at night. Nature is so full of delight. And when it comes to your own thoughts—suppose that you have twenty good thoughts in five minutes, and there's one word in one thought that's absolutely horrible—don't focus on that. Think of things that hold the potential for joy.

It's a practice. You have to learn to separate milk from water. If you give yourself to it, you will be able to watch your contentment grow.

Is there another way to stir up the joy that dwells within us? Yes, there is. In fact, the scriptures are replete with different methods of cultivating joy in order to gain entrance to the highest bliss. The immense compassion of the sages has given us a teaching for every step of the way to God. These teachings are like the comforting hand of a mother, like a raft to save you from floundering in the ocean of birth and death, like a path of light created by moonbeams to lead you through the forest of the world in the dead of night and keep you from getting lost.

In the *Mahābhārata*, the great Indian epic which recounts the triumph of righteousness and joy in a family and a kingdom, there is a wonderful formula for human happiness. It says:

sukhasya mūlam dharma.

The root of happiness is dharma.

Of all the sacred laws of the universe, the highest dharma, the highest duty, is to know one's own Self. The supreme dharma of a human being is to know God.

In the New Testament, in the Gospel of Saint John, Jesus also speaks to his disciples of dharma — righteousness or right action — and its connection to joy. He says, "As the Father has loved me, so have I loved you. If you keep my commandments, you will abide in my love, just as I have kept my Father's commandments and abide in His love. These things I have spoken to you, so that my joy may be in you and that your joy may be full."

The best way to reach the highest dharma, the knowledge of the Self, is to follow the teachings of your Guru. This is what all the Indian scriptures have advocated down through the centuries. By following the teachings of the Master, you reach the pinnacle of joy without a doubt. When you read the lives of all the great saints, you discover the beauty of the Guru-disciple relationship over and over again. You marvel at the mystical bond that unites the two and the incredible joy that wells up in a true disciple's heart whenever he has the opportunity to obey his Guru's command. For that is where the teachings come to life.

For instance, in the *Bhagavad Gītā,* one of the most revered scriptures in Indian philosophy, Lord Krishna gives the highest teachings of yoga to his disciple Arjuna. He tells Arjuna to discard all the limited concepts of his mind and take refuge in the teachings alone. After a great struggle to understand what Krishna was saying, the moment finally came when Arjuna's resistance melted away and he was able to obey Krishna's instructions wholeheartedly. Surely this is what brought the greatest joy to Arjuna.

Following dharma brings you into alignment with the divine will. This effort exists in every mystical tradition. For instance, the great Catholic saint Catherine of Genoa said, "If there is no resistance to the divine will, there is no sorrow either."

So, this is a wonderful *sūtra,* "The root of happiness is dharma." The root of happiness lies in first discerning and then fulfilling your sacred duty at every moment. When you follow the highest path, you reach the highest goal.

According to the sages, good company is another effective way to gather the flowers of joy. The company that you keep tells so much about you. It molds you for better or worse. It can take you to heaven or hell. That means your friends, your colleagues, your chosen companions can either give you life or suck it out of you. The company that you keep can make you the friend of a devil or the friend of God. As Lord Buddha said, "Company with fools, as with an enemy, is always painful; company with the wise is happiness, like meeting with kinsfolk. One ought to follow a good and wise man, as the moon follows the path of the stars."

Of course, in Siddha Yoga, when we talk about company, good or bad, we include the company that you keep inside. Your own positive thoughts are your good company. Your own negative thoughts are your bad company. Since you spend more time with yourself than with anyone else, you have really got to look at what kind of company you are. An outer relationship can be ameliorated—sometimes—with a lot of help. However, the inner work only happens through your cooperation with grace.

For this reason, Baba Muktananda urged seekers to take the support of spiritual practice. In his book *Meditate*, Baba writes, "The purpose of meditation is inner happiness, inner peace. It is fine to have visions, but they are not absolutely necessary. What is necessary is inner joy. When all the senses become quiet and you experience bliss, that is the attainment. The world is the embodiment of joy; joy lies everywhere. Find it and attain it. Instead of having negative thoughts, have the awareness, 'I am pure; I am joy.' Feel good about yourself; fill yourself with great divinity."

All the practices of Siddha Yoga are sources of good company. They keep purifying you until all obstructions disappear and your own divine light flows through you unimpeded. What are the other characteristics of good company? It must have the power to stimulate your intellect positively, bring about a correction in your wrong thinking, and point you in the right direction. The company that you keep should bring you closer to God. The company that you cherish must allow you to bathe in the nectar of your own heart. It must bring you joy.

This evening, we have examined five facets of the teachings of the sages on the *sādhana* of joy: freeing oneself of cravings; the effects of a positive attitude; practicing contentment; following dharma; and cultivating good company, within and without. If you give yourself to these practices, then, one day, as Tukaram Maharaj says, you will swim in the ocean of bliss, that Supreme Reality which lies within each one of us and whose nature is unwavering, imperishable joy. *Nirantara ānanda rasa svarūpam.* It will make you buoyant and support you at every moment of your life. Tukaram says:

> In the great flood of bliss,
> Waves are surging, and they too are nothing but bliss,
> For bliss is the nature of every particle
>   of this body of bliss.

> This is my state. How can I describe this bliss in words?
> Inner delight absorbs me so totally that
> I can never imagine searching for happiness
>   in the external world, through the senses.

> Just as when a child is still in its mother's womb,
> The child's cravings are reflected in the mother
>   and become her desires,

> In the same way, says Tukaram,
> This bliss is reflected throughout my being,
> And whatever comes out of my mouth
> Is an expression of that experience of bliss.

The *sādhana* of joy. With great respect and great love, I welcome you all with all my heart.

December 26, 1994

Chapter Two

THE SADHANA
OF PEACE

With great respect and great love, I welcome you all with all my heart.

Light is the sign of a celebration. At this time of year, especially, you encounter a scintillating flame of light everywhere you turn. The trees are sparkling with strings of lights, the clear night sky is sprinkled with stars and planets glittering like diamonds, and our retreat is brilliantly illuminated by the dancing hearts of the lovers of God. Seekers find it exhilarating to be surrounded by the love of those who rejoice in God's grace. It is such good fortune to have the company of people whose only interest in life is to know God and to serve God.

This is one of the boons of celebrating the birth of a great being. You recognize the blessings of your own life and a mantle of nectarean peace falls over you.

That supreme peace—*śhāntiḥ* in Sanskrit—is the subject of our talk tonight. The Bible calls it "the peace that passes all understanding." It is the experience in which my Guru, Baba Muktananda, lived all the time. Many, many people came to him in their quest for that same peace. Baba always made it clear that supreme peace belongs to everyone. Baba said, "A person turns to religion so he can have true inner peace. The peace that the ancient sages attained within their innermost selves is attainable not only by Hindus, but equally by the followers of the Bible and the *Qur'an*. This is because the peace that spontaneously rises in the heart is essentially the same for all."

"The peace that spontaneously rises in the heart is essentially the same for all." There are three points worth contemplating in this one sentence alone. First of all, Baba calls our attention to the fact that peace is a condition of the heart. Secondly, he says that it arises spontaneously, and thirdly, that the experience of peace is the same for everyone.

Instead of looking for peace where it can be found, people are inclined to seek it in the world outside. They associate peace with certain scenery, or with material circumstances, or even with the escape from responsibility. Have you ever listened to yourself describing the ways you will attain peace? Did you ever catch yourself saying things like:

"If only my husband would help me with the dishes every night, I would be happy."

"If I could only get into that university, my parents would leave me in peace."

"If I only had a body strong enough to meditate for hours and hours and hours, I would never get angry again."

"If I could only climb Mount Meru, I would be satisfied."

"If only I could sit for an hour inside one of those pyramids in Egypt, I know I would find peace."

People always want to believe that peace is a dream come true or a desire fulfilled. It doesn't matter if the dream is simple or outlandish. The point is, it is always an exterior drama. And yet, the result that everyone expects is inner peace. "Peace at last," they say.

Yesterday, two people came up in the *darśhan* line who said they were getting married soon. They were introduced as drama students. That gave me a clue. Falling in love and getting married is wonderful, I told them; and learning drama at school or writing a movie script is also great. However, between the two of them, there must not be any drama; it would only get them into trouble. Even though they are relatively new to this yoga, they understood what I meant. They nodded their heads and smiled. They looked at each other and they agreed.

However, for most people, it is very difficult to come to the conclusion that peace lies within the heart and that is where you really need to look.

Baba also says that peace is spontaneous. People usually think they have to wear themselves out, they have to grind themselves down, they have to run themselves ragged, chasing after serenity. They forget that peace is the grace of the heart. The love of God, the merits of right action, even a moment of right understanding can easily give rise to peace. Whenever the haze that normally clouds your perception gives way and you see your own Self clearly, even for a moment, you experience the most exquisite peace rising up within you. So we can say, if only people will look within, if only people can understand what grace is, then surely they will experience the weariness of life dissolving. They will find themselves gradually becoming anchored in a very natural inner state, one that is calm, free from the agitation of the six enemies, flexible, open to God's will, and intoxicated by the elixir of the heart. Peace is not as rare as you have been led to believe.

When people think about the quest for inner peace, they often think of India. They think of the *mahātmas*, the great souls who live in the Himalayas, the *sādhu bābās*, the renunciants who walk around naked, with matted locks, or who roll in the snow for hours and hours. Somehow people always think peace can be found in a cave, far, far away from crowds and social pressures, not in the so-called world. Nevertheless, Baba Muktananda used to say that he had a lot to teach these *sādhu bābās*, because, in most cases, their attainment was skin-deep;

they had attained nakedness and not much more. Peace lies within and cannot be obtained just by making a show on the outside. Once again, the sages and the scriptures of every tradition ask us to look inside. *Paramaśhāntiḥ*, supreme peace, is a quality of the heart. It is within your grasp, if only you are ready to believe in it.

The third element to contemplate in Baba's statement is his assertion that the experience of peace is the same for all. What an incredible mystical reality that statement reveals! On this globe there is almost endless diversity. Nevertheless, the greater fact is that when it comes to the treasures of the soul, differences vanish.

The arena for duality is the material world of innumerable manifestations, where the senses enact one drama after another. But in the palace of the heart, only one light shines. This light is the same in all beings. Unveiling this Truth, becoming established in the experience of this light, is the goal of spiritual pursuit.

People sometimes ask, "Why must I do *sādhana?*" This is why—to know the Self, to discover the truth of your own nature, within your own heart, for yourself. When you do, you will understand that Baba was not asserting an opinion when he spoke about the oneness underlying the experience of peace. He was stating a simple fact.

Now, you may ask, if inner peace already exists in everyone's heart, why is it so hard to come by? As peculiar as it may sound, there are millions of people in the world who are actually frightened of peace. Does that sound strange to you? Every now and then, you must have experienced it. The fear of being alone, for instance, so alone that you can hear a clock ticking in the next room . . . and, instead of reveling in the peace and quiet, you think, "Oh, I'm scared." The little children in the front row just started laughing. They understand these things very well. Don't you? But we are talking about another kind of peace. As you listen to a little bit more, you will understand.

People are also afraid that they will have to pay too high a price for inner peace. Others look down their noses at the very mention of it. They don't think peace of mind is something they want or need in their lives; they would rather have stimulation. But that's only because they can't conceive of the peace of the Self. Their notions are too superficial.

An even greater number of people are completely unaware of the great peace that lies within them. Still others have pursued tranquility with a thousand different techniques, different paths, traditions, religious rites, therapies, charities, prolonged meditations, severe austerities—the list goes on and on. Understandably, many of them become disappointed after a while, and then they deny the very existence of inner peace.

Baba identified the root of their restlessness, saying, "The more civilized and educated a person considers himself to be, the more agitated he becomes. Other people may regard him as great and praise him, saying, 'How much knowledge he has! What a fine writer! What an excellent scholar!' Still, anxiety and difficulties follow him, and he is without peace. Why does his anxiety keep increasing? It increases because intellectual expansion is based on the notion of duality and difference, and as long as there is duality, there can be no peace."

The lack of inner stillness is directly related to duality. The broken connection between the individual soul and the Supreme Soul, the missing link between a human being and Mother Nature, the hostility between two people—all that is the invention of duality. The result is a restless mind, a mind that panics all the time. You simply cannot experience composure when you are double-minded. You can't sit quietly for a single second if your in-breath and out-breath act as if they've never met.

Duality is more than a concept. It is a perception that is reflected in all your actions.

What is the closest thing to your being? Your own breath.

It is your constant companion. You are alive because of it. The perception of reality begins there, with your breath. When there is unevenness in the breath, as it comes in and goes out, your entire being is disturbed. Of course, you can get so used to living that way that you may not even notice the disharmony under which your whole system is laboring. But it still affects your state of mind, which will look around for reasons to explain its lack of ease. This very simple thing, the flow of air in and out, is often the source of your state. Duality. The problem stems from the inability to experience that it is one breath — within and without, inhaling and exhaling — all just a single movement.

The other great obstacle created by duality is competition: "I want to do better than this one or that one. I want to be greater than so-and-so." This is a source of friction, inside as well as out, and win or lose, it always ends in discontentment. It is a different story if you want to be great in order to inspire others. It is another story if you want to help others and that is what spurs you on. Then these ambitions are the prelude to a wonderful freedom. But how many people can honestly say that this is the case with them?

Duality is the cause of all suffering. It creates incredible tension among people. It generates rivalry and makes the divisions between people wider and wider.

The great yogi and philosopher Bhartrihari wrote many compelling verses about overcoming duality where it begins — in your own perception. He said:

kvachidvīnāvādaḥ kvachidapi cha hāheti ruditam /
kvachidvidvadgoshṭhī kvachidapi surāmattakalahaḥ //

kvachidrāmā gamyāḥ kvachidapi galatkuṣhṭava puṣho /
na jāne samsāraḥ kimamṛitamayaḥ kim viṣhamayaḥ //

What is this world? Is it nectar? Or is it poison?
In one place, you hear music and singing;

In another place, weeping and wailing.
Sometimes you can listen to learned men
    giving discourses;
At other times, your ears are bombarded by
    the quarrels of drunkards.
Sometimes you experience delight in all the pleasures
    the world affords;
At other times, all you experience is your body
    falling apart, covered with sores.
What is this world? Is it nectar or is it poison?

The answer to Bhartrihari's question is that if you seek inner peace, you must constantly work on your perception of the world and other people. You must catch the impulse to see differences and pull it out by the roots. Cultivate a new awareness in its place. What awareness do I mean? Seeing God in each other, seeing unity in diversity, seeing oneness. As Baba always said, "Change the prescription of your glasses. Fill your eyes with knowledge and then perceive the world."

In a contest that was held between two poets in ancient Greece, the question was asked, "What is the best thing for a man, that he may ask it of the gods?" And the chosen answer was, "That he may always be at peace with himself."

There is always an abundance of peace in the universe. From the beginning of time, poets have exalted the peace of the woods, the peace of the sky and the mountains. What else? Looking at the sea fills you with peace. There is immense peace in the sight of an eagle soaring or gliding on the wind. A mountain lake at sunset with a surface that reflects like glass, translucent moving light—all the elements of this world exist in a profound silence, full of peace. Air, water, earth, fire, ether—where is the duality in them?

There is no lack of sweet harmony in the universe. It is only man who is divided within himself, who tears himself apart in conflict, who has no peace.

So the Greek poet gave a very good answer. It also makes a very practical prayer: "Dear Lord, give me the power to be at peace with myself." Otherwise, your conscience is clamoring all the time, eating away at you, imagining all the conceivable consequences of this or that action, perturbing your mind, and contracting your heart. So this is a beautiful blessing to receive from the Almighty, the gift of inner peace.

In his book of aphorisms, *Mukteshwari*, Baba wrote:

> Life is hardly a day.
> Death hovers, counting the minutes.
> Think about life's journey, Muktananda.
> Give up conceit.
> Explore the path of peace.

This is a very beautiful command: "Explore the path of peace." It opens a whole new dimension in our understanding. Peace is not just a passive state, Baba is telling us; it is a territory so vast that it must be explored.

Do you know what else peace is? An ecstatic feast. Peace is not just dessert, it is a full-course meal. Peace is not just the reward, not just the result of spiritual practice, it is an integral part of the process; it is part of the work. You experience serenity even while you are walking the path.

Of course, there is one small hitch. Peace is only available when you are ready to give up your pride. Remember, in his verse Baba spoke of laying aside conceit before he even mentioned peace. Peace is a feast, yes, but one that can only be enjoyed if the senses are silenced. Deep-seated egotistical tendencies must be obliterated and the slate wiped clean if you really want to know the sweetness of the inner state.

Eknath Maharaj was a great poet-saint and scholar of the sixteenth century, who lived in Maharashtra, the region in which our mother ashram in India is set. He was also a householder with a wife and family. While fulfilling all his worldly obligations, Eknath Maharaj realized God. In a magnificent commentary he wrote on the *Shrīmad Bhāgavatam*, Eknath said:

brahmajñānāchī killī, sāṅgate ekacha bolī /
abhimāna nimālī, tūchi brahma //

In just one sentence, I can give you the key
   to the knowledge of the Absolute:
Give up your ego, and then you yourself
   will become the Absolute.

So simple. Just like that. However, the tendencies of the ego are not always obvious. Many years ago, during a question-and-answer session in Gurudev Siddha Peeth, someone complained to Baba about living in a dorm. The remark was not really phrased like a spiritual question. But Baba identified the deeper content and gave a penetrating answer.

The seeker said, "I would like to have a separate room, so that I can remain in isolation. My peace is disturbed by the constant coming and going of people where I live."

Listen to what Baba replied: "Peace cannot be obtained by sitting in a room behind closed doors. In fact, such seclusion sometimes has the opposite effect. By remaining in isolation, you develop tiger-like tendencies. If anyone disturbs a tiger in his cave, he will either leave the cave or attack the intruder. This is not the way to attain true peace. You must learn to remain peaceful and undisturbed in the midst of people."

When it came to the ego, Baba had perfect aim. He always hit the bull's-eye. He's not condemning solitude. On the contrary, Baba was a great lover of solitude, *ekāntavāsa*. He often advised people to spend more time by themselves in order to allow the Shakti within to develop, to contemplate more, and simply to make greater progress in *sādhana*. He used to say that every three months, you should take seven days off and be by yourself—just by yourself, no talking, no mingling with others. Solitude was a practice Baba always cherished, even in the days of his *sādhana*. However, in this particular instance, he was trying to make another point. He was saying that seekers cannot derive any benefit from seclusion unless they first overcome whatever is eating them up from inside. There is no way around it. You must overcome the tendencies that make you want to flee from others.

Sometimes, in the name of *sādhana*, of spiritual life, a person isolates himself or herself from other people. As a result, he becomes insensitive, not just to others but also to the ways of God. Because God does speak through His creatures. When you cut yourself off from whatever you think is disturbing, you actually aren't able to do the *sādhana* of loving God. Instead, what breeds inside you is pretension, arrogance, hostility, a sense of superiority, and so on. And for peace of mind, loving God is so important.

Once there was a great and noble seeker. He had been looking for the Truth for a long, long time. Eventually, he recognized that he could go no further on his own. Just as he was about to despair, someone advised him to go to a particular Master. "He is a wish-fulfilling tree," this friend said. "He will give you what you're looking for. Go to him."

The seeker took this advice to heart. He inquired where the Master lived and set out immediately to see him. He was like a man who thought he was drowning and suddenly discovers the water is not over his head.

Now the Master was omniscient. He knew this noble seeker was coming to see him. So he called the sweeper, the humblest member of his household staff, and he said, "Listen, a certain man will be coming this morning. You've never seen his face before but you will be able to identify him by his fine clothes and the gifts he's carrying. As he comes your way, you must be sweeping very innocently. Bring more dust from other places, put it on the path outside, and when he draws near you, sweep so hard that the dust flies all over him."

The sweeper was very happy to receive a command from her Guru and she ran for her broom. She gathered dust from all over the street. Up the street, down the street, she got a big pile together. She stationed herself a few feet away from the Master's door. When the seeker approached the house, she began to sweep very hard, sending up clouds of dust that coated the seeker from head to toe.

This made the man so angry, he began to call her all kinds of names. She just kept sweeping and sweeping. There was no stopping her. Finally he escaped into the Guru's house. When he was shown into the Master's presence, he fell on his knees and laid his gifts at the Master's feet. Then he folded his hands and humbly implored, "O great Soul, please give me initiation. I am seeking the Truth; I've been searching so long."

The Master didn't even look at him. "You're dirty," he said. "Go to the river. Take a dip and then come back." In fact, this is a ritual which has been followed for centuries. Before you receive initiation, you must bathe; you must purify yourself. You must make yourself worthy.

So the seeker went to take a good bath in the river nearby, and while he was at it, he washed all his clothes very carefully. By the time he left the riverbank, he was immaculate.

Now, the Master called the sweeper once again and said, "He is returning. The same thing, all over again." And that is exactly what happened.

This time, the seeker was beside himself. He just couldn't believe it. He'd been so clean, he'd felt so pure, and he was going to receive initiation. At last! He had been looking for the Truth for twenty-five years, and now that he was on the verge of success, this stupid woman was getting in the way. His pride just couldn't take it. He trembled with rage. He bit back the angry words that rose to his lips and turned away. Brushing himself off, he went inside the Guru's house.

The Guru didn't bother to look at him this time either. He said, "You are still very dirty. You must clean yourself up. For one year, go and get yourself clean, and then come back."

The seeker was heartbroken but he knew he had to follow the command. He had been searching for the Truth for so long, what was one more year? Of course, he could wait. And he did, though the waiting was very hard.

Exactly one year to the day, the same thing happened all over again. The same man, the same sweeper, the same street, the same broom.

Now, you must understand this story took place in the days when there was a caste system in India and sweepers came from the lowest caste. So this was a bigger problem for the seeker than you might think.

This time, the seeker looked at the woman, he looked at the broom, he looked at the dust, he looked at himself, and he nodded his head. He felt just a little irritation. Not much, just a little. He went into the Guru's house without a word.

And the same thing happened. Without even looking at him, the Guru said, "Another year. Purify yourself completely. Come back."

Another year went by. The Guru called the sweeper, "Get your broom. He's coming back."

She got into position, ready to sweep very hard. In fact, the seeker could see her stationed in the road from quite a distance away. This time, he stepped aside. He didn't come anywhere in range of the dust, and as he went around her, he gave her a very sweet smile. He thanked her for all that she had been trying to teach him. Then he went into the house.

The Guru was waiting for him. Everything was ready for his initiation. The Guru looked at him carefully and said, "Yes. Now."

In answer to the person who announced his desire for a separate room in the form of a question, Baba said, "You must learn to be peaceful and undisturbed in the midst of people." This was a teaching Baba imparted over and over again. You must overcome your pride. When you give up your conceit, you will experience deep meditation. When you give up your arrogance, you will know what peace of mind is. Why? Because disturbance does not come from the outside—

not from what people say, not from what people do, not from people's gossip. Disturbance, when it comes, is always the product of your own inner world.

Wouldn't you rather become established in your own treasure instead? The great treasure, inner peace. It is possible to experience serenity all the time, no matter what is going on around you.

In his book *Ashram Dharma*, Baba said, "Study of scriptures, purity of heart and conduct, and simple and unaffected living lead to inner peace."

Let us examine these points one by one.

Study of the scriptures takes you to the pristine world within. By means of the sacred texts, the sages speak directly to you. They teach you how to perceive the world you are living in and how to go beyond the pull of the senses. The scriptures are very practical. They are also tremendously powerful. For example, the *mahāvākyas*, the great statements or utterances of the Vedas, are an endlessly fruitful source of contemplation. There are four of these great statements, each one of which sums up the essential teachings of the Veda from which it comes.

The *Ṛig Veda* declares: *prajñānam brahma*, "Consciousness is Brahman, the Absolute."

The *Atharva Veda* declares: *ayam ātmā brahma*, "The Self is Brahman, the Absolute, the supreme transcendent Reality."

The *Sāma Veda* declares: *tat tvam asi*, "Thou art That."

The *Yajur Veda* declares: *aham brahmāsmi*, "I am Brahman. I am the Absolute."

Each of the major religious traditions also has its own *mahāvākyas*, its own great statements. For instance, the great utterance of Islam is, "There is no God, but God, and Allah is His name."

Judaism declares, "Hear, O Israel, the Lord our God, the Lord is One." The Old Testament also states, "And Thou shall love the Lord God with all thy heart, and with all thy soul, and with all thy might." And, in the book of Leviticus, "Love thy neighbor as thyself."

Some of the principal teachings of Christianity from the New Testament take the form of great statements. For instance, "The Kingdom of God is within you." "Ask and it will be given you. Seek, and you shall find." And, "Do unto others as you would have others do unto you."

The great utterances of Buddhism are called the four Noble Truths. They are: "All existence is suffering." "The cause of suffering is desire." "If suffering has a cause, then it can be removed by removing the cause." "By following the Eightfold Path, the cause of suffering will be removed and *nirvāṇa* will be attained." According to Buddhism, the Eightfold Path consists of right view, right resolve, right speech, right conduct, right livelihood, right endeavor, right mindfulness, and right meditation.

The philosophy of ancient China, called Taoism, declares, "The Tao produced the One, the One produced the Two, the Two produced the Three, and the Three produced the ten thousand things," and, "Meditate on the One."

The ancient philosophy and mystical path known as Kashmir Shaivism says:

iti vā yasya samvittiḥ krīḍātvenākhilam jagat /
sa paśhyansatatam yukto jīvanmukto na samshayaḥ //

He who realizes the identity of the Self
    with the whole universe
And who is constantly united with the Divine,
Views the entire world as the play of the Self,
    which is identical with Shiva.
He is liberated while in the body.
There is no doubt about this.

The teachings of the scriptures add another, deeper dimension to your awareness of the value of life. These are not empty words. They have not come from a limited mind. So they have the capacity to point you toward the light hidden in your own being. They can also expand your understanding of the world you live in. You begin to realize why you are alive.

How can this be? What you are reading in the scriptures is the personal record, the experience of seekers who went across the sea of ignorance. They became known as the sages, the knowers of the Truth, the great ones, the elevated ones. You are reading the wisdom that came from all their effort, inspiration, and sacrifice. These verses are what they heard when they reached the most profound states of meditation. So, when you study the scriptures, what you are really doing is spending time in the company of these great souls. It does give you strength. You find yourself experiencing ethereal peace. Then, instead of drowning in the criticism of other people, you learn what you must learn.

What else did Baba say would lead to inner peace? Purity of heart. So many things happen in people's lives, and they let all of them affect the condition of their hearts. Sometimes, those effects take the form of physical illness, at other times of mental anguish, or cynicism. You may be able to sense it immediately. But just as often, these negative reactions fester for years before they come to the surface, like a low-grade infection that poisons your whole system without your knowing it. So, it is vital for a seeker of the Truth, a seeker of peace, to cleanse his or her heart. Not just once, not just from time to time, or whenever you happen to think of it. The heart must be purified continually. It is a constant *sādhana*.

Chanting is one of the best ways to do this. Letting the divine sound reverberate within you purifies the heart. Baba used to say, the sound of the mantra heals places in you that medicine cannot reach. Tukaram Maharaj chanted incessantly, pouring all the insights of his perfected *sādhana* into songs.

Tukaram sang:

pavitra to deha vāṇī puṇyavanta /
jo vade achyuta sarva kāḷa //

One who repeats the Name of God all the time,
becomes pure in body and his speech is filled with virtue.

I don't know if you've noticed but many people tend to
blurt out whatever is on their minds. There is an old French
expression about this that somebody shared with me:
"Whatever goes through their minds comes out their mouths."
One-way traffic. And this is not just true in France! It's a universal malady. However, if you can check yourself before the
words are spoken, then you will get a genuine insight into the
way your mind works. This in turn gives you a handle on attaining self-control, which is one of the secrets of purification.
Watching your mind, witnessing your mind is a great practice.

Would you like to learn a very reliable technique for cultivating this sort of self-control? Every time a thought arises
in your mind, weigh its worth carefully. Do this screening
process as much as possible in the region of your mind,
before the thoughts and words ever enter the realm of the
tongue. Even then, after they have reached the tongue in their
subtle form, give them a final inspection. Consider once again
the effect these words will have if they become manifest outside your jurisdiction—that is, if they enter the minds of others. Will they be beneficial? Will they wreak havoc? Is that
what you want?

Now you may feel that you are inhibiting yourself by
being so vigilant and so disciplined, and that you have a right
to freedom of speech. But, in the long run, you are doing
yourself a service by exercising some restraint. The people
around you will benefit, too. Do this practice faithfully for a
while and it will become second nature to you. In this way,
you will be making your contribution toward world peace.

Don't you think it will bear great fruit? Yes.

How else can you purify your heart? Intense contemplation is another great way to discard unnecessary thoughts and feelings. It reinforces your foundation in the teachings. Prayer, too, is very cleansing. Someone who can truly pray, who addresses God with an open heart, has made friends with humility. And humility also frees the heart from impurities. So Baba says, purity of heart leads to inner peace. But he doesn't stop there.

Inner peace, he says, also requires purity of conduct. The plot thickens. This is not a very popular thing to say in the modern world. It's not a particularly easy thing for people to hear. Generally speaking, in the guise of freedom of expression, modern opinion promotes an undisciplined life. This does seem to make people feel that they are getting what they want. At least, some people. At least, for a while.

Formerly, all religions and traditions placed more value on right conduct than on giving free rein or license to any old thought, speech, or action. They stressed the importance of behaving with respect toward just about everybody you encountered in life. You were taught to respect your elders, your parents, all women, children, teachers, colleagues, and neighbors, your host when you went out, and your guests when you stayed in.

Do you know what else you were taught to respect? Other people's privacy, other people's possessions, other people's boundaries. You made a point of treating renowned or distinguished people with respect, because of all they had done to make the world a better place, and you also respected scholars and clergymen, brahmins and monks. You extended your compassion respectfully toward the helpless; and to those who came to your aid when you were in trouble, you expressed your respectful gratitude. In fact, you honored practically everything in God's creation.

In the Indian philosophy, you are also taught to show respect to everyone who has ever helped your knowledge to grow or your life to be sustained joyfully. It is said that if someone has taught you even one letter of the alphabet, they are to be respected as your teacher. If you have eaten even a grain of salt in someone's home, you remain eternally grateful. You never, never bad-mouth them.

Nowadays, on the other hand, all of this is being lost. It is gradually disappearing. Under the banner of self-improvement and individual rights, the standards of correct conduct are being tossed away as if they had no value, as if they were no longer relevant. Self-help and self-concern, making people feel they can achieve everything on their own, is the current fashion. In reality, all that has been achieved is the starving of altruism and the fattening, the bloating, of every selfish impulse.

The Indian scriptures declare that if you deflate the false identification with "me, myself, and I," you will attain the awareness of the Supreme Reality and that this awareness sets you free. For example, Jayadevi, a poet-saint from Maharashtra, said:

mai-merā saṃsāra hai, anya nahīṅ saṃsāra /
mai-merā jātā rahe, beḍā hai bhava pāra //

The world consists of the idea of "I" and "mine";
Apart from this idea, no world exists.
Give up the idea of I-ness and my-ness,
And you will have attained liberation.

But these days people are so absorbed in feeding their small self, they miss out on the higher awareness altogether. Children are actually taught to think they don't need God. The result of all this is not surprising. People have no respect for themselves, no respect for the earth, and no respect for each other.

Therefore, the question of right conduct rarely comes up. People make so many excuses, not only for themselves but also for other people's behavior. In the name of being kind and sensitive, they strengthen each other's weaknesses and encourage each other's vices. This, in turn, leads people to commit the very sins from which correct conduct would have saved them. And then they talk about overcoming sin as though it were a mountain that appeared out of nowhere.

Where is all this taking us? People spend a lot of time talking about the end of the world in one form or another. They live with a very vivid sense of impending doom. At the same time, they are hastening their own destruction in a hundred different ways. The fact remains that it is within our power to turn it all around.

Baba Muktananda said, right conduct is the path to inner peace.

One of the stories that Tolstoy wrote is about an angel who disobeyed God. He had been sent to take the soul of a woman to heaven, but out of sympathy for her two newborn babies, he couldn't bring himself to do it. As a result, this angel was exiled from heaven and sent back to earth to learn three truths: what dwells in man, what is not given to man, and what men live by. It took him years to learn those three lessons. Finally, when his experience had ripened into knowledge and he was about to be drawn back to heaven, he spoke of the answers he had found.

Here is a part of what he said: "I knew before that God gave life to men and He desires that they should live. Now I understand more than that.

"I understand that God does not wish men to live apart; and therefore, He does not reveal to them what each man needs for himself. He wishes them to live united; and therefore, He reveals to each of them what is necessary for all.

"I have now understood that though it seems to men that they live by the care they take for themselves, in truth it is love alone by which they live. He who has love is in God, and God is in him, for God is love."

It's interesting that the angel could only learn these lessons on earth. The understanding Tolstoy expresses in this story is very close to the Indian scriptures, which teach that earth is the place where you come to work out all your karma, the consequences of your actions, both good and bad. For that reason, the earth is called *karma bhūmi*, the land of karma. This is where you have the opportunity to learn the greatest lessons and ascend to the highest awareness.

Baba Muktananda said, "This world is called *karma bhūmi* because it gives you the fruit of your actions immediately. . . . Wise beings say that this land is better than hell for sure, but it is also better than heaven or any other plane of existence. Even celestial beings want to take birth in this place. Therefore, man should remember that he has been born in a very beautiful land." Just hearing that, don't you experience peace? You are living in a beautiful land, the earth.

The *Bhagavad Gītā* also makes it clear that a soul does not stay in heaven forever. You are only entitled to enjoy the heavenly realm for as long as your merits last, and merit can only be earned on earth. The *Bhagavad Gītā* says:

*te taṁ bhuktvā svargalokaṁ viśhālaṁ /
kṣhīṇe puṇye martyalokaṁ viśhanti //* [9:21]

Having enjoyed the vast world of heaven,
Souls enter the world of mortals again,
     when their merit is exhausted.

When your good merits are used up, you come back to the earth and here you reap the harvest once again. Therefore, it is so important to examine one's conduct, and be respectful and loving toward one another. Only then can the star of peace shine and beckon to us with its radiance. As a modern Catholic saint once said, "Let us not be justices of peace, but angels of peace."

The final point in Baba's beautiful statement in *Ashram Dharma* is, "Simple and unaffected living leads to inner peace." It is startling to realize how difficult it is to live a life of simplicity and unpretentiousness. For instance, we often hear how the life of a farmer, or life in a village, is filled with harmony and love, compassion and sweetness, generosity and spirituality. In contrast, city life is always described in terms of endless turmoil, anguish, ambition, and adversity. Crime, injury, skepticism, exploitation, and so on—all this is said to be an inevitable part of city life. People go to the countryside and to places of spiritual retreat in search of solitude, simplicity, and nature. However, it is important to remember that your inner world will be reflected outside, no matter where you are. It is very possible to live peacefully in a city and be a nervous wreck on a farm.

If you cultivate inner simplicity, then you can live anywhere and the atmosphere around you will always be serene.

The practice that Saint Teresa of Avila stressed to her students was one-pointedness on God. It was the practice that had brought peace to her soul. On one occasion, she told them, "Let your desire be to see God; your fear, that of losing Him; your grief, that you are not enjoying Him; your joy, that He may take you there. Then you will live in great peace."

Instead of worrying about what you have or haven't got, instead of worrying whether someone else is pleased with you or not, raise the level of your concern. Let it expand. Let it be higher, more beautiful. If you want to have a desire, then let it be a great one. Whenever Baba used to say, "You must overcome all your desires," seekers would ask, "But what about the desire to attain God? What about the desire to attain liberation?" Baba would say, "Ahhh, that's one desire you can keep."

Let your desire be to see God. Always. Whatever you are doing, wherever you are going, with whomever you are speaking, let your deepest wish be, "I want to see God. O Lord, reveal Yourself in this person, in this object, in my dharma, in this action. Whatever I know, whatever I find, may You be there."

It is the same with fear. Instead of being afraid of this or that, have one great fear—the fear of losing God, His presence and His love, of God being veiled and hidden from you. Similarly, grief often wells up, unknowingly, without any reason. Sometimes you're sad and you don't know why. So, if you have to have grief, if you must feel sad, then let it be a sacred grief. Grieve because you are not enjoying God, because you are ignoring Him or neglecting His presence in your life.

In the same way, let your joy be that God is drawing you close. Have this incredible joy bubbling up in your heart: "I have God. One day, I will be one with God. My head will rest on His feet forever and ever." Then you will live in great peace.

In Siddha Yoga, the Guru's grace intensifies your longing for the vision of God. The Guru's grace continually nudges you forward on the path toward oneness. The Guru's grace draws you within to the realm of divine peace. When you become established in this inner experience, when your state can no longer be perturbed, you attain true freedom and supreme peace.

In that ultimate state, the only attachment you have left is to the Guru's feet. There was a modern poet-saint named Tukadyadas, whom Baba knew well during his *sādhana* days. Tukadyadas worked very hard for the cause of national independence, to bring political freedom and peace to the people of India. But the thing on which he placed the most importance was devotion to the Guru, and this is the subject of many of his most beautiful songs. In one of them, Tukadyadas sang:

> How can there be peace of mind without the Guru's grace?
> This is the message of the saints.
>
> You may practice yoga and observe rituals,
> Make endless pilgrimages to temples and shrines;
> Without the Guru, your efforts will be in vain.
>
> Some yogis fast, others meditate in the forest.
> Despite all their austerities, there is no end to their desires.

The company of saints is priceless indeed.

My words may be humble, but they can
Suffuse your life with happiness.

Tukadyadas is absorbed in the Guru's feet.
There is no liberation without them.

Paramaśhāntih, supreme peace, exists in your own heart.
With great respect and great love, I welcome you all with all
my heart.

December 27, 1994

Chapter Three

THE SADHANA
OF LOVE

With great respect and great love, I welcome you all with all my heart.

In his spiritual autobiography, *Play of Consciousness*, my Guru, Baba Muktananda, wrote, "The *sādhana* of love is a very high *sādhana*. Love is also called *bhakti*, devotion. Love is a dynamic and inspiring throbbing of the heart. Love is the very nature of God, whom the scriptural authors have called Supreme Bliss, and *satchidānanda*. It exists in its fullness within man. Even if he does not experience it, it is there nonetheless.

"When a blind man hears others talk about the light, he may say, 'There is no light. I have never seen it. I don't know anything about it.' Yet the light exists; it is only that he has no eyes. Similarly there is love, whether or not it is experienced. If you have not followed the path of love, if you have not tried to find it, how can it be attained?

"Love is a glimpse of the secret inner cave. Love that dwells within flows out through the different sense organs. When it flows to the eyes, it makes forms beautiful; when it flows to the ears, it makes sounds melodious; when it rises to the tongue, it makes tastes sweet and pleasing."

We have come together once again to drink the elixir of

divine love. Nectarean love. Supreme love. Unconditional love. Love is the magnet that draws God's attention.

So, yes, tonight our subject is the *sādhana*, the spiritual path and practice, of love. We are going to focus on God's love, and on our love for God. What difference is there? Isn't love itself the experience of oneness, of union with the Absolute Reality? Isn't pure love the very body of God?

One of the definitions of love in the dictionary is of interest to us tonight. It says that love is "the benevolence attributed to God, as resembling a father's affection for his children." It also says love is "men's adoration of God in gratitude or devotion." In other words, we are the children of God. The other day in *darśhan*, someone said, "Today for the first time I feel that I am the child of God. For so many years, I heard it said, but I was really only hearing about it. Today, for the first time, I know it's true."

Love is a key word in every language. Still, it is also true that love comes in many forms. Love has so many different shades, colors, branches, and ramifications. In this world, love stretches from birth all the way to death like a range of hills. Some near, some far. Their variety alone captures the imagination. Most people spend their lives wandering through these hills, these paths of love. They go up and down, in and out, high and low.

Each hill looks different from the others, doesn't it? Oh, it's so fascinating, so intriguing. A mother's love, romantic love, platonic love. Isn't love bewitching? What a view! Isn't it inviting? So alluring, you can't resist it—and so gratifying. The love of work, the love of food, the love of danger. Oh, it's so exciting, so thrilling. Love is overwhelming. Isn't it? The way people love their pets. The way they love their car. The way they love their computer! You name it and love's there.

Most of you have probably gone through a lot of these different hills yourselves, the ups and downs of love. You are so used to the terrain that you continually expect a high or a rush in the name of love, and you are always bracing your-selves against the landslide of disappointment that hits you on the way down.

Is that it? Is that all there is to love? Not really. There is another kind of love. It is the sole possession of those who seek God. It is love for God alone. It has no dips and fluctua-tions. It is not fickle either. Constancy is its very nature, and it never fades, because its source is ever-new.

Worldly people have trouble understanding this kind of love. The South Indian poet-saint Akkamahadevi explains that it is because they don't go deep enough. She says:

Would a circling surface vulture
 know such depths of sky
 as the moon would know?

Would a weed on the riverbank
 know such depths of water
 as the lotus would know?

Would a fly darting nearby
 know the smell of flowers
 as the bee would know?

O Lord White as Jasmine
 only you would know
 the way of your devotees:
 how would these,

these
 mosquitoes
 on the buffalo's hide?

The love she is describing, *parābhakti*, is difficult to attain. Ultimately, however, this love alone endures. It lasts through all eternity. To become that kind of devotee, to have supreme love course through the heart without ceasing, great spiritual practices must have taken place. Only after your little limited individuality has been thoroughly annihilated do you know what the love of God really is. Only then are you light enough to ascend to the realm of love. A great effort is required. A great choice must be made. A great price must be paid. For this love is beyond description.

In his *Bhakti Sūtras*, the classical text on devotion, the divine sage Narada says:

anirvachanīyam premasvarūpam // [51]
mūkāsvādanavat // [52]

The nature of divine love is inexpressible.
It is like the experience of joy that a mute man has
    when he tastes something sweet.

Since the glory of *parābhakti* cannot be described, the wisest and most beneficial thing you can do is learn to apply the experience of divine love to your daily life. Baba Muktananda was the perfect example of this. Every gesture he made, every word he spoke was an expression of his love for God. That is why the slightest contact with him, even the slightest thought about him, fills you with the experience of that same love. Baba once said, "In your ordinary life, learn to love. This love should be pure, unattached, and given for its own sake. If it contains any demands, it is just a commercial exchange—the motions of love, but not love itself."

Don't think that somehow if you surround yourself with more and more and more love from the world, you can make yourself a better person. Don't fool yourself by thinking that you can keep losing yourself in the hills and valleys of worldly love and somehow everything will be all right. Trying to gather more and more of this kind of love, which is filled with attachments, is like walking on thin ice — you just never know. Of course, you can go a long way before the ice splits and you sink into the chilling *māyā* of despair. However, without the intervention of grace — which is another name for God's love — you are fighting a losing battle with your senses, without wearing any armor or carrying the shield of God's protection.

Why don't you let your heart steep in the elixir of divine love instead?

In South India, in the twelfth century, there was a gathering of devoted hearts in a tradition of Shaivite worship and practice. The heart-piercing poems, or *vachanas*, of the saints of this tradition speak of divine love and the longing for God with an intensity and directness that startles you. For Basavanna, one of these great saints, the devoted heart is the only hope. He says:

> Does it matter how long
> a rock soaks in the water:
> will it ever grow soft?
>
> Does it matter how long
> I have spent in worship,
> when the heart is fickle?
>
> Futile as a ghost
> I stand guard over hidden gold,
>
> O Sangameshwar, Lord of the Meeting Rivers.

In many old stories, where there is a treasure hidden, there is also a ghost to protect it. In other stories, the apparition can be a divine messenger.

Something like this happened to Ibrahim, who was the king of the ancient land of Bokhara and also a true seeker of God. Ibrahim was fascinated by the company of saints and sages. He loved to listen to them talk about the Lord and the spiritual path. On the other hand, he adored wealth and luxury. Wherever Ibrahim went, forty gold swords were carried in front of him, and he slept on a bed strewn with fragrant flower petals, six inches thick — gardenias, roses, jasmine.

Now one night while he was asleep in his luxurious bed, Ibrahim was awakened by a very rough sound, a rumbling, scuffling noise that was coming from the roof right above his chamber. So he got up and went to investigate. He found two men stomping around on the roof.

"What are you doing up here?" said the king.

"O, sir," one of them replied, "we are camel drivers and we are looking for our lost camels."

The king was amazed at their stupidity. He said, "Are you crazy? How could you ever expect to find your camels on the roof of the palace?"

One of the men turned to him and said, "In the same way, Your Majesty, that you hope to find God while lying on a bed of flowers." With these words, the two men disappeared into the night.

The king was shocked. The longing that had been smoldering inside him for so long began to catch fire. He couldn't sleep all night, and the next morning, when he went to hold court, he was still very pensive and troubled. He sat on his throne, listening to the business of state in a restless, distracted mood. Petitioners bowed before him and mumbled their requests. And he said yes or no, granting their wishes or refusing them, without really listening. Then, suddenly, a man he had never seen before walked right up to the throne and stood in front of him. That got his attention.

"What do you want?" said the king.

"Oh, I just stopped at this inn for a while."

"*Inn?* This is no inn! This is my palace!" the king said indignantly.

"Oh really? Who owned it before you?" said the man.

"My father, of course."

"And before him?"

"My grandfather. Naturally."

"And before him?"

"Well, his father," said the king.

"And where did they all go, when they left?"

"They're dead."

"Ahh," said the man. "Then is this not an inn which one man leaves and another man enters?" And with that, the stranger bowed and walked away, vanishing into the flock of petitioners and attendants at the entrance of the room.

"Wait," said Ibrahim. But the man was gone.

The fire blazed even more fiercely in the heart of the king. It was not a comfortable feeling. Bewildered, he got up and walked out of the room himself, telling his courtiers, "Send them all home. I'm going hunting. This has been a very strange day."

He set off on his favorite horse, riding as fast as he could across the hills, accompanied by his entourage. But it was almost as if he didn't know what he was doing or where he was going, because, somehow, without noticing, he became separated from his troops. Now the external situation was a perfect mirror of his mood: he was lost and he was on his own.

As he galloped along, he suddenly heard a voice cry out. *"Awake!"*

The king pretended he had not heard. He rode on even faster. Then he heard it a second time. *"Awake!"*

Still the king refused to pay any attention. He whipped his horse and urged it to go faster.

A third time the voice rang out. *"Awake! Before you are struck awake! Time is running out!"*

At that moment, a deer appeared a little way down the path. Ibrahim obstinately prepared to chase it. But instead of running away, the deer turned, looked him in the eye and said, *"Awake! Or is it just for this that you were created?"*

The king turned his face away from the deer, but then he heard the same word coming from his saddle. *"Awake!"* And then the voice seemed to come from right within his own robes. *"Awake!"* It felt as if his own soul were calling out to awaken him from *samsāra*, the world of appearances. He wanted to run, but where could he go to escape a message that was coming from inside him? Suddenly the heavens themselves seemed to split apart with a sound like thunder. His head fell back. The gates of his heart were flung open and he found himself weeping with the love of God.

The next day the king put his most trusted minister on the throne and left the palace. He set off in search of a Master, for he no longer wanted to live as a stranger to the inner kingdom of his own heart.

It is the work of the saints to awaken people from *samsāra*, the world of the wandering, from this *chakra*, this wheel, the cycle of birth and death. One of the most beautiful songs on this subject was written by the poet-saint Kabir, who became, legend tells us, the Guru of the king of Bokhara. Kabir says:

> Awake, O my dear friend, wake up!
> Why do you go on sleeping?
> The night is over—
> Do you want to lose the day in the same way?
> Those who are awake find a priceless jewel.
> How foolish you are to miss your chance
> by sleeping the sleep of ignorance!
>
> Kabir says, only they remain awake
> whose hearts have been pierced
> by the arrow of the divine Word.
> Wake up, my dear friend! Wake up!

Baba Muktananda attained *parābhakti*, supreme devotion, through his intense love and surrender to his own Master, Bhagawan Nityananda, whose grace is never-ending. It was Baba's experience that without the intervention of grace, life is a long dull sleep. Without grace, one is without real love. And without love, what is a human being? Baba once said, "Without peace, without love, a *sādhu* is zero, a yogi is zero, a wise man is zero, a lecturer is zero, and a scholar is zero. Therefore, one should have this uninterrupted awareness all the time. What is this unbroken awareness? It is to become established in 'I am That,' having attained the right understanding of it." *So'ham,* the natural, spontaneous mantra, "I am That."

Without the experience of inner love, without embracing God's love, without the *darśhan* of one's own true nature, without the awareness of *So'ham,* "I am That," a human being is like an empty container. When Baba says "zero," he means a person is completely devoid of the understanding of his own true worth. Baba used to say, it doesn't matter how many zeroes you have, they are meaningless unless you put a number "one" in front of them.

When you experience God's love for you and your love for God, you acquire the missing number. Otherwise, your life is of no consequence, no matter what your status in society may be. Without love, you're just an empty zero. As Allama Prabhu, one of the ecstatic South Indian poet-saints, sang:

If mountains shiver in the cold
with what
will they wrap them?

If space goes naked
with what
shall they clothe it?

If the Lord's men become worldlings
where will I find the metaphor?

O Guheshwara, Lord of the Caves.

Like Kabir, isn't Allama Prabhu crying out to awaken us to the uninterrupted vision of the Truth? Isn't he urging us to have an unceasing awareness of love? Isn't that the source of all attainments?

So, Allama Prabhu says, O Lord, You who dwell in the cave

of the heart, when your people become completely absorbed in the *māyā*, the illusion of the world, what analogy can I find for them? I don't even know what to call them. What should I say they are? What is their state?

You can't attain anything without devotion. It is like preparing a wonderful dessert, but leaving out the sweetness. No sugar, no modern chemical substitute, not even a healthfood sweetener. It's like collecting a whole library full of books, but never opening a single one. So all that wisdom remains on the shelf, nothing but a pompous show. It is like practicing austerities and carrying them to an extreme, making a display of your heroic discipline, with a heart that is numb to the glory of God. How can such cold discipline bear fruit?

This does not mean that you should throw away your books or abandon discipline. Certainly not. It means that you should add the love of God to everything you do. Just as the people in the dining hall put on gloves before they serve the food, call on the love in your heart before every action you perform.

Adding devotion to spiritual practices, it is said, is like adding fragrance to gold. This is one of the phrases that the saints use all the time. The dryness of the heart can only be moistened with God's love. A life that is not drenched in *bhakti* grates like sandpaper. Without devotion, all your encounters with people, the way you deal with the circumstances of your daily life, all your conversations and perceptions are coarse and abrasive, filled with arrogance. It's only devotion that softens everything and adds *rasa*, juice, flavor, to life. Love makes life worth living.

When you receive *śhaktipāt*, divine initiation from the Guru, your *kuṇḍalinī* energy is awakened within. Your eyes are opened to an inner world that you never knew existed. You see familiar things in a new way. You see new sights with the innocence and wonder of a child. Sometimes this can be very subtle. Still the miraculous begins to envelop your existence; and you cannot tell if all this beauty is coming from the inside out, or the outside in. You begin to perceive shimmering stars of light—not only in your meditation and chanting sessions, but also while you eat, while you perform any of your daily activities. You may think it is just a fleeting glimpse of the Divine—a star flashes before you and disappears; or it plays with you by darting here and there in the world around you. Yet, it is an indication that grace has awakened you from within and is beginning to show you the world, and life in the world, as a play of consciousness.

This afternoon, around one o'clock, the sky was clear and the sun was shining very brightly. Out of nowhere, dark clouds gathered, and in what seemed no time at all, they completely covered the sky, soaking up the light. Thick drops of rain began to fall, as big as hailstones, pounding and bouncing on the ground. Some people thought we were in for a blizzard. But no, before you knew it, the sun was shining brightly and there wasn't a single cloud in the sky.

What a play—a play of consciousness, a play of divine light. If you watch it with devotion, your heart is filled with gratitude. You savor the ambrosia of great love. It permeates your whole being and the environment around you. As your *sādhana*, your spiritual work, continues, you become more and more anchored in this region of light, in the abode of love.

Baba Muktananda described the vision of devotion quite precisely. In *The Perfect Relationship*, his book on the Guru-disciple relationship, Baba wrote, "The bliss that springs from the awareness and vision of oneness is that which I call devotion. It is the essence of all knowledge and yoga. That blissful vision of oneness is like the unbroken showers that make the rain clouds and the ocean appear as one."

Oneness, the ability to experience unity in diversity. The whole purpose of yoga is to erase the small "I" and expand one's awareness until it is capable of attaining *pūrṇo'ham*, the pure "I," the perfect "I." This purified sense of self is free from all egotistical tendencies. It is untainted by worldly attachments. It is beyond petty dualities, beyond attraction and aversion, beyond likes and dislikes, beyond gain and loss. It is perfect oneness with all things, and its nature, its *svarūpa*, is *prema*, pure love.

To experience perfect love, you must have perfect surrender. How can you receive a gift if your hands are full or your fists are clenched? How can you reach the ocean of love if you only go in the direction of suffering? How can you hope to rise to nobility of spirit when you spend your time with a low-minded person who is obsessed with his own degraded goals and values? As Baba often said, if you plant lemons, don't expect mangos. Finally, what makes you think that you can attain divine love by clinging to your ego, as if it were nectar instead of poison, as if it were life instead of death?

Total love comes from dissolving your small will into God's all-encompassing heart. Total love comes from total surrender. Akkamahadevi, another South Indian poet-saint, experienced that level of perfect surrender. Listen to her song:

If sparks fly
I shall think my thirst and hunger quelled.

If the skies tear down
I shall think them pouring for my bath.

If a hillside slides on me
I shall think it flowers for my hair.

O Lord White as Jasmine, if my head falls from my shoulders
I shall think it Your offering.

What a sublime experience. Of course, no one says the path of love is easy. Never. No one says the *sādhana* of love is smooth. Never, never. There are hardships: simple hardships, and also difficult ones. There are sacrifices: great sacrifices, small sacrifices. There are challenges: little challenges, big challenges. There is a tremendous struggle. You try to hold on to your accumulated beliefs, no matter how much you aspire to God. Definitely, the individual's idea of himself is the highest and most perilous mountain to cross. Your ego is your worst enemy.

Sometimes on the path of love, you almost feel so ripped apart, you are afraid there won't be enough of you left to taste a drop of God's love. Sometimes you are filled with such unbearable darkness, only your own warm tears running down your cheeks let you know that you're still alive. Absolutely, there is no doubt about it, the path of divine love leads through a high and treacherous land.

You must be fearless to attain *parābhakti*, supreme love. In the words of Mahatma Gandhi, "A coward is incapable of exhibiting love. That is the prerogative of the brave."

The Upanishads say, only a courageous one will know the Self. And, as Akkamahadevi said, you must be willing to give everything for the experience. She said:

Look at
love's marvelous
ways:

> if you shoot an arrow,
> plant it
> till no feather shows;

> if you hug
> a body, bones
> must crunch and crumble;

> weld,
> the welding must vanish.

Love is then
our Lord's love.

In the art of glassblowing, the craftsman must use extremely intense heat and flame in order to shape the molten liquid into the most delicate and captivating forms. When this process is occurring, the temperature climbs so high that the liquid hardly looks like glass. Do you know how hot a fire must be to melt and fashion glass? In Fahrenheit, it must reach 1,562 degrees; in Celsius, 850 degrees. Furiously hot!

Now, what do you think? When you say you are "burning" in *sādhana*, how hot is it? Shall I tell you? The fire of love is a million times stronger. It is wondrous!

Saint Catherine of Genoa described this fire in her poetry. The way she captured the experience in words is breathtaking. Listen:

> When God sees the Soul pure, as it was in its origins,
> He tugs at it with a glance,
>   draws it and binds it to Himself with a fiery love
> that by itself could annihilate the immortal soul.
> In acting thus, God so transforms the soul in him
> that it knows nothing other than God;
> and He continues to draw it up into His fiery love
> until He restores it
>   to that pure state from which it first issued.
>
> These rays purify, then annihilate.
> The soul becomes like gold
>   that becomes purer as it is fired,
> all dross being cast out.
>
> Having gone to the point of twenty-four carats,
> gold cannot be purified any further;
> and this is what happens to the soul
> in the fire of God's love.

I love this poem. I have read it many times. It is so true. The devotional saints of South India also expressed this experience very beautifully. Akkamahadevi sang:

O mother, I burned in a flameless fire
O mother, I suffered a bloodless wound
Mother, I tossed without a pleasure:
loving my Lord White as Jasmine
I wandered through unlikely worlds.

The poet-saint Allama Prabhu said:

It was
    as if the fire in the tree
    burned the tree

    as if the sweet smells
    of the winds of space
    took over the nostrils

    as if the doll of wax
    went up in flames

I worshipped the Lord
and lost the world.

A Sufi mystic sang:

In love, there is no difference between life and death.
We live for our Beloved, and we are always dying
    for our Beloved.

Like the other saints in this devotional tradition, Basavanna imparted the highest mystical teachings about *bhakti* in his poetry. He said:

Don't you take on
this thing called *bhakti*:

    like a saw
    it cuts when it goes

    and it cuts again
    when it comes.

If you risk your hand
with a cobra in a pitcher
will it let you
pass?

Like love, the purifying fire takes several forms. One of
them is meditation. Baba used to describe the meditation cave
in the Gurudev Siddha Peeth ashram in India as a furnace of
meditation. Anyone who went to Baba and said, "I can't get
into meditation," or, "I can't sit still," was told to go sit in the
cave. "Go to the furnace of meditation," he'd say. Invariably,
they fell into meditation there.

In fact, on many occasions, Baba said that all of Gurudev
Siddha Peeth was like a furnace. Wherever you walk in that
ashram, you experience the fire of *parābhakti*. You look at a
tree and you begin to weep. You see that love. You go and sit
on a rock; you feel yourself melt with love. You go to the
samadhi shrine, and before you know it, your heart has dissolved
from the sublime closeness you feel with Baba. You go to the
chant; you have hardly opened your mouth and you are in
ecstasy. You are a true drunkard. You go to do your seva;
before you know it, the task has been done. Why? How can
you account for such an ongoing miracle?

In his book *Ashram Dharma*, Baba said, "An ashram
manifests the divine glory. Here the radiant blazing Chiti Shakti
carries on Her sublime work. The ashram may appear to be
an ordinary place to our physical eyes, but its every leaf,
flower, fruit, tree, and creeper is pervaded by the Kundalini
Shakti. Therefore, one should live here with vigilance in
thought, speech, and action."

The image of fire is rich and very meaningful. It implies
intensity, the power of illumination, the power to burn away
impurities, a quality of being that is inherent in everything—
for everything has the capacity to burn. In India, tradition-
ally, a corpse is cremated. So fire is also seen as the bridge

between the worlds. When we speak of "the fire of love," we are speaking of union with God.

On one of Baba's first trips to Australia, an archdeacon of the Church of England asked, "Would Baba expect that all people all over the world are the same?"

Baba replied, "Yes, that's what I believe. Everyone is the child of God."

"Would you also say that all religions are the same?" the minister continued.

And Baba answered, "All religions are valid to me because the light of God is in every one of them. The founder of every religion is a man of God, an ideal man, and he gathers a large number of followers because of the ideals which his character reveals. I am always saying that we must not be distracted by individual differences, differences of personality, and differences of the *guṇas* or qualities of nature. We should look directly at the Self, which is the same in everyone. Riches, poverty, literacy, illiteracy, these are all external things and do not affect the internal reality of man which transcends these distinctions."

Love knows no distinctions. Every heart blazes with the divine light. Every heart trembles with divine love. Even if a person is unaware of his own yearning, every human being is constantly engaged in the pursuit of lasting happiness, profound peace, and unconditional love. After searching endlessly in the transitory things of this world for something that will produce these states of being, each person must eventually turn around and look within. This is the truth, without a doubt. All goodness springs from within. All of God's treasures and miracles are hidden within the heart of everything that lives.

In his ecstasy, the Sufi saint Mansur Mastana expressed his teachings in sublime songs. His words are challenging. Sometimes it almost seems as if he is daring seekers to venture into the intoxicating territory of mystical love. Many of you already know his song *Agara hai śhauka milane kā*. You are welcome to join and sing it with us. For those who have never heard it before, let me tell you the refrain first. Mansur Mastana says:

agara hai śhauka milane kā, to hara dam lau lagātā jā /
jalākara khudanumāī ko, bhasama tana para lagātā jā //

If you really long to meet God,
Then direct all your love toward Him.
Burn up your ego in the fire of love,
And smear its ashes on your body.

The *bhasma*, the three stripes of ash that yogis put on their foreheads before worship or meditation, signifies the same thing. It represents the ego burnt in the fire of love. We wear it as a reminder that the Supreme Self lies beyond the ego. The rest of Mansur Mastana's song goes like this:

Take hold of the broom of love
And sweep your heart clean of the filth of duality.
Brush the dust away from your place of worship.

Always eat and drink this love; never, never neglect it.
Roam in your own inner intoxication.
Never run from the fire that is burning up your ego.

Become neither a Muslim priest nor a brahmin priest.
Stop worshiping duality.
This is the command of the Emperor of all:
Constantly make this declaration: 'I am God! I am God!'

Mansur Mastana says, I have recognized Him,
I have seen Him in my own heart.
This is the tavern of ecstatic beings.
Let this be the center of all your movements.

The *sādhana* of joy, the *sādhana* of peace, and the *sādhana* of love. Every evening of our retreat has been filled with great devotion. The knowledge of the heart, the wisdom of the great Self. Every day you have been waking up in grace, living in grace, and going to sleep in grace. Every morning the sky has shown its glory.

When the Sun rises, the Moon and Venus seem to draw even closer to each other. These days both of them have been clearly visible, very close, and shining brilliantly in the heavens. In the Indian tradition, the Moon represents the mind, and Venus represents love. So, all along, as we have performed our spiritual practices, our seva, we have been soaking in the elixir of divine love. Let us continue to perform our dharma with this understanding.

Many people have said that they have been experiencing so much kindness, so much politeness, so much compassion among people in this retreat. "What is it? What has made this retreat so special?" they ask. Somehow it seems that the planets and the stars are coming into harmonious alignment. Similarly, seekers are coming into alignment with the Shakti, the great energy, with grace, and with the teachings of the Siddhas. As you drink in the teachings more and more, you do become filled with *parābhakti*, supreme devotion.

Now, whatever you do, do it with love. As a thought arises in your mind, check—is there love in it? When you're about to speak a word, stop yourself and check—is there love in it? Whatever you are going through in your life, great suffering or supreme bliss, ask—is my heart longing for God? Is my heart drenched in God's love? Where do I stand in my relationship with God?

Remember: Wherever you are, God is. We all live in God's heart. The *sādhana* of love.

With great respect, with great love, I welcome you all with all my heart.

Sadgurunāth Mahārāj ki Jaya!

December 28, 1994

NOTE ON SOURCES

Many of the quotations from scriptures have been freshly rendered, drawing from the following sources in English, in addition to the original Sanskrit texts:

Karapatri Swami. "Sri Shiva Tattva," *Sanmarga*. Benares, 1946, as quoted in *Hindu Polytheism*, by Alain Danielou, New York: Pantheon Books, 1964

Sharma, Arvind. *Our Religions*. San Francisco: Harper San Francisco, 1993

The following quotations are reproduced by permission of the publishers:

All quotations from Jnaneshwar's commentary on the Bhagavad Gita are from *Jnaneshwar's Gītā*, rendered by Swami Kripananda. Copyright © 1989 by State University of New York. Reprinted by permission of SUNY Press.

Verse from the *Atharva Veda* from *The Vedic Experience: Mantramanjari*, translated and edited by Raimundo Panikkar. Copyright © 1977 by Raimundo Panikkar. Reprinted by permission.

Poetry of Akkamahadevi, Basavanna, and Allama Prabhu from *Speaking of Śiva*, translated by A. K. Ramanujan. Copyright © 1973 by Penguin Books Ltd. Reproduced by permission of Penguin Books Ltd.

Poetry of Catherine of Genoa reprinted from *Catherine of Genoa*, translated by Serge Hughes. Copyright © 1979 by The Missionary Society of St. Paul the Apostle in the State of New York. Used by permission of Paulist Press.

GUIDE TO SANSKRIT
PRONUNCIATION

Vowels

Sanskrit vowels are categorized as either long or short. In English transliteration, the long vowels are marked with a bar above the letter and are pronounced twice as long as the short vowels. The vowels 'e' and 'o' are always pronounced as long vowels.

Short:	Long:
a as in c*u*p	*ā* as in c*a*lm
i as in g*i*ve	*ī* as in s*ee*n
u as in f*u*ll	*ū* as in sch*oo*l
e as in s*a*ve	*ai* as in *ai*sle
o as in ph*o*ne	*au* as in c*ow*
ṛi as in w*ri*tten	

Consonants

The main variations from the way consonants are pronounced in English are the aspirated consonants. These are pronounced with a definite *h* sound. In particular, *th* is not pronounced like the English *th*, as in *th*rone, nor is *ph* pronounced as in *ph*one. They are pronounced as follows:

Aspirated Consonants:	Other Consonants:
kh as in ink*h*orn	*ṅ* as in si*ng*
gh as in lo*gh*ut	*ñ* as in ca*ny*on
jh as in he*dg*ehog	*ṇ* as in no*n*e
ṭh as in boa*th*ouse	*n* as in s*n*ake
th as in an*th*ill	*ś* as in bu*sh*
ḍh as in roa*dh*ouse	*ṣ* as in *sh*un
dh as in a*dh*ere	*kṣ* as in au*ct*ion
ph as in loo*ph*ole	*ṃ* is a nasal *m*
bh as in a*bh*or	*ḥ* is an aspiration

For a detailed pronunciation guide, see *The Nectar of Chanting*, published by SYDA Foundation.

85

GLOSSARY

Abhanga(s) [*abhanga*]
A devotional song composed in the Marathi language, expressing the longing for God.

Abhinavagupta [*abhinavagupta*]
(10th-11th century) One of the most revered and mysterious of the great Siddhas of Kashmir Shaivism, he wrote more than 60 works. These include tantras, definitive works of aesthetic theory, devotional hymns, and, in the later part of his life, profound commentaries on the philosophy of the Pratyabhijna School (the Doctrine of Self-Recognition). He synthesized all the various strains of Shaivism of his time in works that are remarkable for the beauty of their language and the profundity of their thought. His masterwork is generally considered to be the *Tantrāloka* (*Light of the Tantras*), a massive undertaking in thirteen volumes. *See also* Paramarthasara.

Akkamahadevi [*akkamahādevī*]
(12th century) Also known as Mahadevi Akka (elder sister); an ecstatic poet-saint of South India. She was the younger contemporary and disciple of the great Shaivite saint Allama Prabhu. She composed many devotional poems (*vachanas*) in the Kannada language, in which she addresses Shiva as *Chenna Mallikarjuna*, "the lovely Lord White as Jasmine"— a form of Shiva she fell in love with in the temple at Udutadi where she was born.

Allama Prabhu [*allama prabhu*]
(12th century) A great Shaivite saint of South India, also known as Prabhudeva, the Master. He presided over a huge gathering of Shaivite saints — all of whom considered him to be their Guru — in what came to be known as "The Mansion of Experience." He composed many beautiful devotional poems (*vachanas*) in the Kannada language, in which he honors Shiva, in the form of his own Guru, as *Guheshwara*, Lord of Caves.

Arjuna [*arjuna*]
Third of the five Pandava brothers and one of the heroes of the *Mahābhārata*; considered to be the greatest warrior of all. He was the friend and devotee of Lord Krishna. It was to Arjuna that the Lord revealed the knowledge of the *Bhagavad Gītā. See also* Mahabharata.

Ashram [*āshrama*]
(*lit.*, a place that removes the fatigue of worldliness) The abode of a Guru or saint; a monastic place of retreat where seekers engage in spiritual practices and

study the teachings of yoga.

Atharva Veda [*atharva veda*]

One of the four primary scriptures of India (which were *shruti*, "heard," by inspired *rishis*, seers). Protective healing formulas and prayers predominate in the *Atharva Veda*. *See also* Rig Veda; Sama Veda; Vedas; Yajur Veda.

Baba Muktananda

See Muktananda, Swami.

Baba/Babaji [*bābā/bābāji*]

(*lit.*, father) A term of affection and respect for a saint, holy man, or father. *See also* Muktananda, Swami.

Basavanna [*basavanna*]

(1105-1167) Named after Lord Shiva's vehicle, Basavanna was a political activist and social reformer who became the king's treasurer as well as a leading Virashaiva poet-saint. At 16, he left home and entered a holy temple of Sangameshwar, where the waters of three rivers meet. Here, he served his Guru, his deity, "the Lord of the Meeting Rivers," until in a dream, Lord Shiva appeared and sent him to Kalyan to serve the king. Devotees flocked to be in Kalyan, under his spiritual direction, in a huge gathering of saints that came to be known as "The Mansion of Experience." In addition to his poetry (*vachanas*), he is known for establishing the eight distinctive features of Virashaiva practice.

Bhagavad Gita [*bhagavad gītā*]

(*lit.*, Song of the Lord) One of the world's spiritual treasures; an essential scripture of Hinduism; a portion of the *Mahābhārata*, in which Lord Krishna instructs his disciple Arjuna on the nature of God, the universe, and the Supreme Self; on the different forms of yoga, on the nature of dharma, and on the way to attain liberation.

Bhagawan [*bhagavān*]

(*lit.*, the Lord) One endowed with the six attributes or powers of infinity: spiritual power, righteousness, glory, splendor, knowledge, and renunciation. A term of great honor. Swami Muktananda's Guru is known as Bhagawan Nityananda. *See also* Nityananda, Bhagawan.

Bhagawan Nityananda

See Nityananda, Bhagawan.

Bhakti [*bhakti*]

The path of devotion described by the sage Narada in his *Bhakti Sūtra*; a path to union with the Divine based on the continual offering of love and the constant remembrance of the Lord. *See also* Narada.

Bhakti Sutras [*bhakti sūtra*]

The classical scripture on devotion composed by the sage Narada; also known as the *Philosophy of Love*. *See also* Bhakti.

Bhartrihari [*bhartṛihari*]

(5th century) A legendary renunciant, poet, and sage; a king who gave up his throne to become a yogi; the collection of his poems is known as the *Shatakatrāyam*.

Bhasma [*bhasma*]

Ash from the sacred Vedic fire ritual (*yajña*), charged with the power of mantra, that is used by yogis, swamis, and devotees to draw three white horizontal stripes on the forehead and other parts of the body to represent the limitations that are reduced to ash by *sādhana* and the power of grace. One of the most auspicious and ancient of Shaivite practices.

Brahman [*brahman*]

(*lit.*, expansion; swelling of spirit) Vedantic term for the Absolute Reality. The Supreme Being without form or attributes. *See also* Satchidananda; Upanishads; Vedanta.

Brahmin [*brahmin*]

A Hindu priest, scholar, or teacher.

Catherine of Genoa, Saint

(1447-1510) Born into an aristocratic Italian family, Catherine underwent a profound religious experience ten years after her marriage. At the age of 26, she and her husband together devoted their lives to working at a hospital for the poor. She became hospital director from 1490-96, and it was during this time that she received a series of mystical visions. Her *Purgation and Purgatory* is an account of her understanding, through meditation and revelation, of the transformation of the self through the love of God.

Chandogya Upanishad [*chāndogya upaniṣhad*]

One of the principal Upanishads from the *Sāma Veda*, it lists and illustrates, through dialogue and legends, the three requirements of dharma (duty): to sacrifice or give alms, to practice austerities, and to become the student of a true Master. *See also* Sama Veda; Vedas.

Chidakasha [*chidākāśha*]

The subtle space of Consciousness in *anāhata* (the subtle energy center of the heart) and *sahasrāra* (the center at the crown of the head), sometimes described as the sky of Consciousness.

Chidvilasananda, Swami [*chidvilāsānanda, swāmī*]

(*lit.*, the bliss of the play of Consciousness) The name given to Gurumayi by Swami Muktananda when she took the vows of monkhood.

Chiti Shakti [*chiti śhakti*]

The power of universal Consciousness; the creative aspect of God portrayed as the universal Mother, the Goddess.

Darshan [*darśhan*]

A glimpse or vision of a saint; coming into the presence of a holy being; seeing God or an image of God.

Dharana(s) [*dhāraṇā*]

(*lit.*, holding; bearing; keeping in remembrance) A technique for centering the mind and preparing it for meditation that is described in the *Vijñāna Bhairava*; also, concentration: the sixth stage of yoga described by Patanjali in the *Yoga Sūtras*.

Dharma [*dharma*]

Essential duty; the law of righteousness; living in accordance with the divine Will. The highest dharma is to recognize the truth in one's own heart.

Eknath Maharaj [*eknāth mahārāj*]

(1528-1609) A householder poet-saint of Maharashtra, the author of several hundred devotional songs (*abhangas*) in the Marathi language. He was expelled from the brahmin caste because of his attempts to abolish untouchability. By writing on religious subjects in the vernacular, Eknath ushered in a spiritual revival among ordinary people. A revered example of discipleship, he often referred to himself as "Janardan's Eknath," placing the name of his Guru, Janardan Swami, before his own.

Ganeshpuri [ganeshpurī]

A village at the foot of the Mandagni Mountain in Maharashtra, India. Bhagawan Nityananda settled in this region where yogis have performed spiritual practices for thousands of years. Gurudev Siddha Peeth, the ashram which Baba Muktananda constructed at his Guru's command, is built on this sacred land. Gurumayi spent many of the years of her *sādhana* here. The samadhi shrines of Bhagawan Nityananda in Ganeshpuri and Swami Muktananda at Gurudev Siddha Peeth attract many thousands of pilgrims.

Guheshwara

See Allama Prabhu.

Gunas [guṇa]

The three essential qualities of nature which determine the inherent characteristics of created things. They are *sattva* (purity, light, harmony, and intelligence); *rajas* (activity and passion); and *tamas* (dullness, inertia, and ignorance).

Guru [guru]

(*lit.,* gu, darkness; ru, light) A spiritual Master who has attained oneness with God and who is therefore able both to initiate seekers and to guide them on the spiritual path to liberation. A Guru is also required to be learned in the scriptures and must belong to a lineage of Masters. *See also* Shaktipat; Siddha.

Gurudev Siddha Peeth [gurudev siddha pīṭha]

(Siddha Peeth, *lit.,* abode of perfected beings) The main ashram of Swami Chidvilasananda and of Siddha Yoga in Ganeshpuri, India. It is the site of the samadhi shrine of Swami Muktananda. Charged with the power of divine Consciousness, the ashram is a world-renowned center for spiritual practice and study. *See also* Ganeshpuri.

Gurumayi [gurumayī]

(*lit.,* one who is absorbed in the Guru) A term of respect and endearment often used in addressing Swami Chidvilasananda.

Guru's feet [guru]

The Guru's feet appear in most Indian scriptures, where they are said to embody Shiva and Shakti, knowledge and action, the emission and reabsorption of creation. Vibrations of the inner Shakti flow out from the Guru's feet. They are a mysterious source of grace and illumination, and a figurative term for the Guru's teachings. This is why many beautiful and ancient hymns are addressed to them and to the Guru's sandals (*pādukās*), which are also said to hold this divine energy of redemption and enlightenment.

Hari Giri Baba [hari giri bābā]

A Siddha from Vaijapur, Maharashtra, who bestowed great love and affection on Swami Muktananda during his *sādhana* days in Yeola and Suki. He was famous for filling the pockets of the many coats he wore with pebbles, picked up as he walked ecstatically along the riverbanks.

Himalayas [*himālaya*]

The tallest range of mountains in the world (located along the border of India and China), which is considered to be the sacred abode of yogis, sages, and gods.

Intensive

A program designed by Swami Muktananda to give direct initiation into the experience of meditation through the awakening of the *kuṇḍalinī* energy. *See also* Shaktipat.

Jayadevi [*jāyadevī*]

A poet-saint of Maharashtra, whose songs Swami Muktananda collected during the days of his *sādhana*, and about whom very few personal details are known.

Kabir [*kabīr*]

(1440-1518) Also known as Kabir Sahib or Kabirdas, a great poet-saint, who lived the simple life of a weaver in Benares. His followers included both Hindus and Muslims, and his influence was a powerful force in overcoming the fierce religious factionalism of the day. Bracing and penetrating, ecstatic and sobering, his poems describe the experience of the Self, the greatness of the Guru, and the nature of true spirituality. They are still being studied and sung all over the world.

Karma [*karma*]

(*lit.*, action) The consequences of our verbal, mental, or physical actions, out of which our destiny is made. There are three categories of karma: that destined to be played out in this lifetime; that which is reserved for future lives, currently stored in seed form; and the karma being created in the present lifetime.

Kashmir Shaivism

The sublime philosophy of non-dualism that recognizes the entire universe as a manifestation of one divine conscious energy; a branch of the Shaivite philosophical tradition that explains how the formless Supreme Principle, Shiva, manifests as the universe. Together with Vedanta, Kashmir Shaivism provides the basic scriptural context for Siddha Yoga.

Krishna [*kṛishṇa*]

(*lit.*, the dark one; the one who attracts irresistibly) The eighth incarnation of Lord Vishnu, whose life story is told in the *Shrīmad Bhāgavatam* and the *Mahābhārata*, and whose spiritual teachings, as related to Arjuna on the battlefield, are known as the *Bhagavad Gītā*.

Kundalini Shakti [*kuṇḍalinī śakti*]

(*lit.*, kundalini, the coiled one; shakti, spiritual power) The Supreme Power, primordial energy, that lies coiled in a dormant state at the base of the spine in every human being. When awakened, this extremely subtle force, also described as a goddess, travels upward through the many channels of the subtle body, initiating various yogic practices and purifying the whole system. When purification is complete, Kundalini becomes established in the *sahasrāra*, the spiritual center in the crown of the head. There, the individual self merges into the Supreme Self, and the cycle of birth and death comes to an end. *See also* Intensive; Shaktipat.

Lord Krishna.

See Krishna.

Lord of Caves
See Allama Prabhu.

Lord of the Meeting Rivers
See Basavanna.

Lord White as Jasmine
See Akkamahadevi.

Mahabharata [*mahābhārata*]
An epic poem in Sanskrit, composed by the sage Vyasa, which recounts the struggle between the Kaurava and Pandava brothers over a disputed kingdom. Within this vast narrative is contained a wealth of Indian secular and religious lore. The *Bhagavad Gītā* occurs in the latter portion of the *Mahābhārata*.

Maharashtra [*mahārāshtra*]
(*lit.,* the great country) A state on the west coast of India. Many of the great Indian poet-saints lived in Maharashtra; the samadhi shrines of Bhagawan Nityananda and Swami Muktananda are also located in this region, which both of them loved and lived in for many years.

Mahatma(s) [*mahātma*]
(*lit.,* great soul) A term of respect often used to describe the solitary ascetics and yogis who perform their austerities in the mountains.

Mahavakya(s) [*mahāvākya*]
(*lit.,* great statement) Four statements containing the wisdom of the Upanishads, asserting the oneness of the individual Self and God: *aham brahmāsmi* (*Yajur Veda*); *ayam ātmā brahma* (*Atharva Veda*); *prajñānam brahma* (*Rig Veda*); *tat tvam asi* (*Sāma Veda*).

Mansur Mastana
(858-922) Also known as "al-Hallaj." An ecstatic Sufi poet-saint who lived most of his life in Baghdad. He also journeyed through Iraq, Persia, Gujarat, and Kashmir to the periphery of China. He was hanged as a heretic for his pronouncement *Ana'l Haq*, "I am God," which orthodox Islam of those days would not tolerate, and became famous forever after among Muslims and the lovers of God as "the martyr of mystical love."

Mantra [*mantra*]
(*lit.,* sacred invocation; that which protects) The name of God; sacred words or divine sounds invested with the power to protect, purify, and transform the individual who repeats them.

Maya [*māyā*]
The power of illusion; the indefinable power of the supreme Being that projects the illusion of the universe; ensnaring power.

Mount Meru [*meru*]
A mountain in the Himalayas, considered in ancient India to be the center of the earth.

Muktananda, Swami [*muktānanda swāmī*]
(1908-1982; *lit.,* the bliss of freedom) Gurumayi's Guru, often referred to as Baba. Born into a devout and prosperous family in South India, he left home at 15 to begin his spiritual journey. After taking the vows of monkhood, he traveled throughout India for 25 years, studying the major branches of Indian philosophy and yogic science. His spiritual longing was not satisfied until

he met the great *siddha* Bhagawan Nityananda, who gave him *shaktipāt*, spiritual awakening. After nine years of intense spiritual practices, he attained Self-realization. In 1961, before Bhagawan Nityananda left his body, he transferred the power of the Siddha lineage to Swami Muktananda. At his Guru's command, Baba brought the powerful and rare initiation known as *shaktipāt* to the West during three world tours in the 1970s. As the inheritor of a great lineage of spiritual Masters, he introduced the path of Siddha Yoga all over the world, creating what he called a "meditation revolution." Baba made the scriptures come alive, teaching in words and action, by example, and by direct experience. His message to everyone was: Honor your Self, worship your Self, meditate on your Self. Your God dwells within you as you.

Murti [*mūrti*]

(*lit.*, embodiment; figure; image) A representation of God or of a chosen deity which has been sanctified by worship. A *mūrti* can be both a symbolic embodiment of the presence of God, as in a *shivaliṅga*; or a recognizable human figure, as in the image of a saint.

Narada [*nārada*]

A divine *ṛishi*, or seer, who was a great devotee and servant of Lord Vishnu. He appears in many of the Puranas (ancient legends) and is the author of the *Bhakti Sūtras*, the authoritative text on *bhakti yoga*. See Bhakti; Bhakti Sutras.

Neti neti [*neti neti*]

(*lit.*, not this, not this) The steady negation of all unreal aspects of oneself and

the world that is practiced by Vedantins. *See also* Vedanta; Vedantins.

Nirvana [*nirvāṇa*]

Liberation of the soul from the effects of karma and bodily existence; the state that follows the cessation of desire and illusion; the attainment of Truth.

Nityananda, Bhagawan [*nityānanda bhagavān*]

(d. 1961; *lit.*, the lord of eternal bliss) Swami Muktananda's Guru, also known as Bade Baba (Big Baba). He was born a Siddha, living his entire life in the highest state of Consciousness. Little is known of his early life. He came from South India and later lived in Maharashtra, where the village of Ganeshpuri grew up around him. He spoke very little, yet thousands of people experienced his grace. His samadhi shrine is located in the village of Ganeshpuri, a mile from Gurudev Siddha Peeth, the principal ashram of Siddha Yoga. *See also* Bhagawan.

Paramarthasara [*paramārthasāra*]

(*lit.*, the essence of the highest goal) A short, 11th-century treatise on Kashmir Shaivism written by the great saint Abhinavagupta. In 100 verses, he describes the nature of bondage and the process of liberation through *shaktipāt*, the descent of grace. *See also* Abhinavagupta.

Paravani [*parāvāṇi*]

The deepest level of sound, emanating from supreme Consciousness. From here, sound arises successively through the causal and subtle levels of consciousness, until it manifests on the gross level as *vaikhari*, or articulated speech.

Prasada [*prasāda*]

A blessed or divine gift; often refers to food or other items that have first been offered to God and later distributed.

Rasa [*rasa*]

Nectar, flavor; a subtle energy of richness, sweetness, and delight.

Rig Veda [*ṛig veda*]

One of the four Vedas, the *Ṛig Veda* is composed of over one thousand hymns of wisdom, containing some of the world's greatest poetry; this Veda is intended for the priest whose function is to recite the hymns inviting the gods to the fire rituals. See also Vedas.

Rudra [*rudra*]

A name of Lord Shiva meaning "Lord of Tears." A figure of unbearable radiance, bright as the midday sun, sometimes also called "The Wild God," Rudra has been revered since Vedic times as the source of all: Creator, Sustainer, and Destroyer. As the fierce aspect of God, the name of Rudra inspires great love and great fear among his worshipers. See also Shiva.

Rumi, Jalaluddin

(1207-1273) The most eminent Sufi poet-saint of Persia and Turkey, the father of the Mevlavi order of Sufis, and one of the greatest spiritual poets of all time. After meeting Shams-i Tabriz, an ecstatic wandering saint, he was transformed from a sober young scholar into an intoxicated singer of divine love. His major works are the poetry of the *Divani-i-Shams-i Tabriz*, and the monumental collection of his teachings called the *Mathnavi*.

Rupees [*rupee*]

A small unit of Indian currency.

Sadgurunath Maharaj ki Jaya! [*sadgurunāth mahārāj ki jaya*]

(*lit.*, I hail the Master who has revealed the Truth to me) An exalted, joyful expression of gratitude to the Guru for all that has been received.

Sadhana [*sādhana*]

A spiritual discipline; practices on the spiritual path; for example, contemplation, meditation, mantra repetition, chanting, and offering oneself in selfless service.

Sadhu(s)/sadhu baba(s) [*sādhu bābā*]

A wandering monk or ascetic; a holy being; a practitioner of *sādhana*.

Sahasrara [*sahasrāra*]

The thousand-petaled spiritual energy center (*chakra*) at the crown of the head, where one experiences the highest states of consciousness. It is the seat of Lord Shiva, the supreme Guru. When the Kundalini Shakti reaches this center and unites with Lord Shiva, the meditator achieves the state of enlightenment, or Self-realization. See also Kundalini Shakti.

Sama Veda [*sāma veda*]

One of the four Vedas, the *Sāma Veda* is a liturgical collection of hymns sung to melodies of great beauty. See also Vedas.

Samadhi shrine [*samādhi*]

The tomb of a saint; after their *mahā-samādhi* (*lit.*, the great *samādhi* or final union with the Absolute), great yogis and saints are buried seated in a yogic posture, surrounded by precious and sacred objects. Pervaded by rays of their divine love and wisdom, the saints' resting places are tended with the utmost reverence as centers of prayer and meditation, and a source of blessings for all who come there.

Samsara [*samsāra*]

The world of change, mutability, and death; the world of becoming; the cycle of birth and death.

Satchidananda [*satchidānanda*]

(*lit.*, absolute Existence, Consciousness, Bliss) The three indivisible categories used in Vedantic philosophy to describe the experience of the Absolute.

Self, the

Divine Consciousness residing in the individual; described as the witness of the mind, or pure I-awareness; the *ātman*, described in Vedantic philosophy as identical with Brahman, the Absolute.

Seva [*sevā*]

(*lit.*, service) Selfless service; work offered to God, performed with an attitude of nondoership and without attachment.

Shakti [*shakti*]

Force, energy; spiritual power; the dynamic aspect of supreme Consciousness that creates and maintains the universe. *See also* Kundalini Shakti.

Shaktipat [*shaktipāt*]

(*lit.*, the descent of grace) The transmission of spiritual power (*shakti*) from the Guru to the disciple; spiritual awakening by grace. *See also* Kundalini Shakti.

Shankaracharya [*shankarāchārya*]

(780-820) One of the greatest philosophers and sages of all time. He spread the philosophy of absolute non-dualism (Advaita Vedanta) throughout India. In addition to teaching and writing, he established ashrams in the four corners of the country. The order of monks to which Swami Muktananda and Swami Chidvilasananda belong was created by Shankaracharya. *See also* Vivekachudamani.

Shiva [*shiva*]

In Kashmir Shaivism, the Self of all; the all-pervasive, unchanging, transcendent Consciousness; in the Hindu trinity in which Brahma is the creator and Vishnu is the sustainer, Shiva is the third aspect of God: the destroyer of ignorance.

Shrimad Bhagavatam [*shrīmad bhāgavatam*]

One of the Puranas, it consists of ancient legends of the various incarnations of the Lord, including the life and exploits of Lord Krishna, and stories of the sages and their disciples.

Siddha(s)/Siddha Guru [*siddha*]

A perfected yogi; one who lives in the state of unity-consciousness and who has achieved mastery over the senses and their objects; one whose experience of the Supreme Self is uninterrupted and whose identification with the ego has been dissolved. *See also* Guru.

Siddha Yoga [*siddha yoga*]

(*lit.*, yoga of the perfected beings) A path to union of the individual and the Divine that begins with *shaktipāt*, the inner awakening by the grace of a

Siddha Guru; also known as *mahāyoga* (*lit.*, the great yoga), because *śhaktipāt* initiation sets in motion a spontaneous and intelligent process in which any or all forms of yoga will occur within the seeker according to need and temperament. Swami Chidvilasananda, Swami Muktananda's chosen successor, is the living Master of this path. *See also* Guru; Kundalini Shakti; Shaktipat.

Six enemies

The inner enemies spoken about in Vedantic philosophy: desire, anger, delusion, pride, greed, and envy.

So'ham [*so'ham*]

(*lit.*, I am That) The natural vibration of the Self, which occurs spontaneously with each incoming and outgoing breath. By becoming completely aware of this mantra, which is constantly repeating inside of us, a seeker is able to experience oneness with the Self.

Sufi

One who practices Sufism, the Islamic mystical path of love, which teaches that the goal of life is realization of the divine Principle in the heart.

Sutra [*sūtra*]

A scriptural verse or phrase.

Teresa of Avila, Saint

(1515-1582) A Spanish Catholic mystic and a woman of commanding personality. She founded and supervised 17 convents in a period of 20 years, traveling all over Spain. A classical example of someone who combines an intensely contemplative life with practical activity and common sense, she recorded the results in books, the most important of which are an autobiography, written at the request of her confessors, the *Way of Perfection*; the *Book of Foundations*; and *The Interior Castle*.

Tukadyadas [*tukādyadās*] or Tukadoji Maharaj [*tukādoji mahārāj*]

[20th century] A poet-saint from Maharashtra, India; a contemporary and a friend of Swami Muktananda; and later, a beloved figure in the political struggle for Indian independence. During the days of Muktananda's *sādhana*, the two great yogis often chanted together the many *bhajans* or devotional songs that Tukadyadas composed about the spiritual path and devotion to the Guru.

Tukaram Maharaj [*tukarām mahārāj*]

(1608-1650) A great householder poet-saint of Maharashtra. He received initiation in a dream and wrote thousands of devotional songs (*abhangas*) describing his spiritual experiences, his realization, and the glory of the divine Name.

Upanishads [*upaniṣhad*]

(*lit.*, sitting near) The inspired teachings, visions, and mystical experiences of the ancient sages, or *ṛishis*, of India. These scriptures, exceeding 100 texts, constitute "the end" (*anta*) or "final understanding" of the Vedas; hence the term Vedanta. With immense variety of form and style, all of these texts give the same essential teaching, that the individual soul and God (Brahman) are one. *See also* Vedanta.

Vachanas [*vachana*]

(*lit.*, saying, thing said) Devotional

poems written in the Kannada language by the Virashaiva saints of South India. In this innovative free verse, breaking away from the established tradition of formal Sanskrit, men and women of every class, caste, and trade speak about Shiva and speak directly to Shiva. *See also* Akkamahadevi; Allama Prabhu; Basavanna.

Vasishtha [*vasiṣṭha*]

The legendary sage and Guru of Lord Rama. Vasishtha epitomized the force of spiritual knowledge. He is the central figure of the *Yoga Vāsiṣṭha*, which is one of the most rigorous scriptures on the nature of the mind and the way to free it from illusion. *See also* Yoga Vasishtha.

Vedanta [*advaita vedānta*]

(*lit.,* end of the Vedas) One of the six orthodox schools of Indian philosophy; the philosophy of absolute nondualism, exemplified by the Upanishads and other texts that consider the nature of the Self. *See also* Upanishads; Vedas.

Vedantin(s)

Follower(s) of Vedanta.

Veda(s) [*veda*]

(*lit.,* knowledge) Among the most ancient, sacred, and revered of the world's scriptures, the four Vedas are regarded as divinely revealed eternal wisdom. They are the *Atharva Veda, Ṛig Veda, Sāma Veda,* and *Yajur Veda.*

Vijnana Bhairava [*vijñāna bhairava*]

An exposition on the path of yoga based on the principles of Kashmir Shaivism. Originally composed in Sanskrit, probably in the 7th century, it describes 112 *dhāraṇās,* or centering exercises, which give the immediate experience of union with God. *See also* Kashmir Shaivism.

Vivekachudamani [*vivekachūḍāmaṇi*]

(*lit.,* the crest jewel of discrimination) An 8th-century philosophical Sanskrit commentary on Advaita Vedanta written by Shankaracharya, it expounds the teaching that Brahman, the Absolute, alone is real. It is considered to be a prime example of the philosophical genius as well as the spiritual attainment of this great Siddha Master. *See also* Shankaracharya.

Yajur Veda [*yajur veda*]

An eternal scripture whose hymns specify sacrificial formulas and rites and the rules for their correct performance, which are said to control the harmonious functioning of the universe. *See also* Vedas.

Yoga [*yoga*]

(*lit.,* union) The spiritual practices and disciplines that lead a seeker to evenness of mind, to the severing of the union with pain, and through nondoership, to skill in action; ultimately the path of yoga leads to the experience of the Self. *See also* Siddha Yoga.

Yoga Vasishtha [*yoga vāsiṣṭha*]

Also known as *Vāsiṣṭha Rāmāyaṇa.* A very popular Sanskrit text on Advaita Vedanta, probably written in the 12th century, and ascribed to the sage Valmiki. In it, the sage Vasishtha answers Lord Rama's philosophical questions about life, death, and human suffering, by

teaching that the world is as you see it
and that illusion ceases when the mind
is stilled.

Yogi(s) [*yogī*]
A practitioner of yoga, who through the
practices of yoga attains higher states of
consciousness. *See also* Yoga.

INDEX

Further Reading

Swami Chidvilasananda
My Lord Loves a Pure Heart
Kindle My Heart
Ashes at My Guru's Feet

Swami Muktananda
Ashram Dharma
Play of Consciousness
From the Finite to the Infinite
Where Are You Going?
I Have Become Alive
The Perfect Relationship
Reflections of the Self
Secret of the Siddhas
Selected Essays
I Am That
Kundalini
Mystery of the Mind
Does Death Really Exist?
Light on the Path
In the Company of a Siddha
Lalleshwari
Mukteshwari
Meditate

You may learn more about the teachings and
practices of Siddha Yoga Meditation by contacting:

SYDA Foundation
371 Brickman Rd.
South Fallsburg, NY 12779-0600, USA

Tel: (914) 434-2000

or

Gurudev Siddha Peeth
P.O. Ganeshpuri
PIN 401 206
District Thana
Maharashtra, India

For further information about books in print by Swami Muktananda and
Swami Chidvilasananda, and editions in translation, please contact:

Siddha Yoga Meditation Bookstore
371 Brickman Rd.
South Fallsburg, NY 12779-0600, USA

Tel: (914) 434-0124